DIS–
CONNECTED

DIS—
CONNECTED

HOW TO STAY HUMAN
IN AN ONLINE WORLD

EMMA GANNON

Andrews McMeel
PUBLISHING®

CONTENTS

INTRODUCTION

WHEN I THINK ABOUT THE BEAUTY OF CONNECTION, I THINK ABOUT trees. Bear with me—I'm not asking you to hug them while wearing tie-dye and holding crystals (yet). But I do think we can all learn, during a time of utter chaos, how trees (said to be the oldest-living organisms on the planet) communicate with each other. In 1997, ecologist Suzanne Simard discovered that trees "communicate their needs" and "send each other nutrients," even sending "warning signals" about environmental changes to each other.[1] They keep each other in the loop, they stay connected, they compete sometimes but also protect each other. They use their network of roots to cooperate and help each other. Like the trees, whether we like it or not, we are all connected, even more so now through our screens and social media networks, and our actions have consequences on each other. We have the power to cooperate and help each other or cut each other off. The harsh reality is, like the trees, we actually have the power to make each other sicker or stronger. Humans often treat trees as if they are disposable, but without them there would be no "us." Without trees, all hope would be lost. Without each other, we would be lost too. We need each other more than ever. Be it climate change, a loneliness epidemic, or a global COVID-19 pandemic, the world is in crisis. Fear can make us pull away from each other when, really, we need to do the opposite. We could do with a good hug (human or tree, your choice).

Like the trees, we have our own global network—a network of billions made up of many different people at different points in life. The wiser, older trees have more knowledge and stronger roots—we also grow deeper into who we are with knowledge and age. We've lived online for a while now, and it is no longer a shiny new toy. Perhaps we are going into our next phase. This book is about how we can connect better online, using the network we have at our fingertips, which we may often take for granted. A network that never ceases to amaze me: the good, the bad, and the ugly. How quickly we can rally together in times of need, and how quickly we can drag something down. We have the power to make or break things, including each other. When I first started writing this book, I thought I was going to write a book about how hyperconnected to everything we are yet at the same time worryingly disconnected from each other.

That is still partly what this book is about, but more crucially
I realized it is a book not just about how disconnected we are
from each other but more so from *ourselves*. The more individualistic our culture gets, the more we disconnect from each other
and lose sight of a more common goal. Ironically, the more we
obsess about our own individualism (how we look, how we
are perceived, what we can get), the more we lose touch with
our true individuality and how we can make a difference. With
so much at our fingertips—so many choices, so many images
whizzing past, so many distractions, so many algorithms, so
many advertisements—we are in danger of forgetting who we
are, what we like, what we want from life. The things that we
love, the conversations we want to have, the lives we want to
live. The internet, when used without a plan, can embed us
further and further into the depths of man-made culture, full
of distraction techniques, dodgy money schemes, and virtual
arcade machines, and we could risk losing touch with our own
human nature. We could be in danger of spending our lives
engulfed in someone else's online game and missing out on the
small moments of joy that happen to us every single day. We
can either choose to use the internet to further real connection
or use it to hide away and numb everything out.

At the beginning, we were promised an internet world that
would help us change things for the better—at least that's what
I naively believed. The internet would help us educate and be
educated, be a tool for everyone to access the knowledge they

needed; social media was to be a place to connect people and start social movements. In 2011, for example, it was said that Twitter played a pivotal role in the Arab Spring, amounting to more than two million tweets a day; Facebook was said to be "reviving dormant relationships"; and the *Guardian* wrote about how children with internet access were being given a huge advantage. A decade later, we are at a turning point, a point in time when we can reflect on what the internet has brought us up until now and decide how we want to use it for the better. When I google "how to improve our internet experience," all I am met with is *harder better faster stronger* tips on getting a better internet connection or router. Boost your internet speed! Click here for time-saving internet advice! Hack your way to success! No, no! I'm asking: How do we have a better *experience*, as humans, using these tools we plug into every single day? When I ask, "How do we have a better time online?" I'm really asking, "How do we have a better experience of life when so much of it is spent online?" The two things aren't as separate as we once thought they were. The internet really is our life now. Online and offline life aren't separate entities. How we act online also reflects who we really are. Time for a big reflection, rest, reboot. After all, most of us can't just log off forever—and I wouldn't want to, either. When I am using it intentionally, the internet can be a completely magical gift enhancing all areas of my life.

For so long, the internet was my portal to another life, a digital career, fascinating people, creative minds, life lessons, and travel inspiration. It felt like being inside a big arcade, pulling levers and not knowing what treat you might get. I could crack jokes with someone halfway across the world on Twitter, instead of talking to a boring housemate who I had nothing in common with. I could make money by not leaving the house. I could find out something huge about the history of the world that I was never taught at school. I could teach myself how to edit audio, or take care of a plant, or fix my headphones via a YouTube tutorial. Fast-forward to now. I feel sick at how much of my life it's taken up without me really stopping to think. I feel sick at how many ocean views I have looked at through my phone's camera lens instead of my own eyes. It was in 2016 that I wrote a book called *Ctrl Alt Delete: How I Grew Up Online*, in which I wrote about my love affair with the online world. I was an internet kid, and proud of it. Millennials are/were lucky—we grew up alongside the beginning of the internet instead of being catapulted immediately into TikTok-land the moment we were born. We posted pixelated photos, didn't have many filters, were limited by a computer curfew and slow, loud dial-up—just one shared PC in a household with rules about how long we could spend on it. We were the first "digital native" generation. No wonder we are questioning our long, rocky relationship with the internet now that we are adults.

The internet and the instant connection it brings have been sources of great positivity for me: I've made friends for life (including, for example, a Twitter friend who lives in Los Angeles and who I met up with IRL five years ago—thankfully she hadn't catfished me—and who years later I invited to my wedding); I have built a successful business, both emotionally and financially (and still live nomadically when I can with just my laptop in a tote bag); and I constantly still find myself connecting with thousands of like-minded people who make me feel fulfilled in my work. However. There was a time, mainly during my twenties, when I grew more dependent on the characterization and output of my "online self" and my connection to my devices, and I grew apart from who I was away from all of this. The amount of time I spent online building my brand and growing a community made me forgetful and distracted and ended up taking me away from the person I wanted to be. It took me away from my core relationships. I forgot birthdays, I was a terrible friend, I was zoned out. I was making more effort impressing strangers than nurturing relationships with those who truly love me for me. I felt distanced from myself, the person who had once had hobbies and enjoyed simple pleasures, who liked dancing and having picnics and listening to the birds. I was focused on growing followers and showcasing a polished exterior. If I'd had an "inner child," she would have been screaming at me to take a break, sit quietly, and reconnect with her. I was so addicted to growing my outwardly successful "online self," feeding the hamster-wheel reward system of online validation, that I had momentarily lost track of the basics of my core being. As Dante calls it, I was climbing "Mount Delectable"—getting more and more rewards, collecting more and more career trophies to post online, but, you guessed it, I was less happy and more lonely. Now, I look at people who spend a lot of time outwardly peacocking and showboating their successes online and pause to question how they are really doing.

A few years ago, I was invited by the Oxford Union at Oxford University (gulp) to debate the topic "Does social media corrupt human interaction?" I was paired up with TV presenter Cherry Healey, and we debated "for" the proposition in front of a live audience. I listed reasons why social media was alienating us from each other, including a mind-bogglingly high statistic about the number of people who had checked their phone *during* sex, which got a laugh. We argued that social media projection allows us to hide the truth of our real selves and thus inhibits real connection. We won the debate. Even though social media has brought me so many good things, it is clear that it has many qualities that mean we are moving further and further away from true human connection.

It makes me concerned for teens. I had a Nokia brick phone when I was thirteen, so there was only so much damage that could be done on a phone that hardly got a signal. Of course, so much of adolescence is universal regardless of tech, and bullying absolutely occurred even in Nokia-land. But we can't ignore that an increase in platforms could mean an increase in issues. According to the Mayo Clinic, "social media use can also negatively affect teens, distracting them, disrupting their sleep, and exposing them to bullying, rumor spreading, unrealistic views of other people's lives and peer pressure. A 2019 study of more than 6,500 12- to 15-year-olds in the U.S. found that those who spent more than three hours a day using social media might be at heightened risk for mental health problems."[2] We have to admit that, although there are so many positive elements of online life, it is still a Wild West for a lot of people of all ages.

Looking at the online network I had in my twenties, who were my real friends and who were my acquaintances? I had accidentally mixed everything up. Why was I putting so much trust into people I'd only met a handful of times online? Why wasn't I putting more time into my lifelong friendships? What would a perfect day look like for me without knowing what anyone else was up to? I would ask myself: What songs do I actually want to listen to, without a targeted prompt from Spotify? What books do I want to read, without Amazon telling me I might like them? What clothes do I truly want to wear, without the influence of a trendy blogger with a discount code? What do I want my house to look like, outside of Pinterest-y house-porn Instagram accounts? I love the internet for the creative inspiration it gives me, but I also felt as if I was morphing into someone who depended on people's approval before checking in with myself, my own tastes, opinions, feelings, emotions, and directions.

Yes, we can blame the tools themselves for the endless distraction, keeping us so busy and engulfed in notifications that we are growing distant from ourselves and sometimes people around us. However, we also need to look at ourselves. There is something to be said for how we might *quite like* the endless, easy excuses and distractions, or the constant ability to reach for our phones and laptops whenever we want. It's a place to get lost in, an easy place to numb out and ignore some of the not-so-fun parts of life. It's a cozy comfort blanket that we can pull over our heads when things get too much. We can definitely partly blame the engineers who build the addictive prompts that keep us constantly connected, but I do think we need to unpick what part we also play in it. As Oliver Burkeman said in a recent newsletter, "Yes, it's true we live in a system that demands too much of us, leaves no time for rest. . . . But it's also true that we're increasingly the kind of people who don't *want* to rest—who get antsy and anxious if we don't feel we're being productive."[3] I moan about how people don't take my "out of office" seriously. About how tethered I am. About how I can't catch a breath, and how "always on" everything is. So, I need to do better at disconnecting myself, then. I need to set boundaries. I need to not be resentful. I can't keep blaming everyone else. We have choices and boundaries we can set. You have agency over your own life. We get to say no. We get to change our habits. It's not easy—it never is—but the first step is acknowledging the problem.

The disconnection and subsequent loneliness caused by my addiction and absorption into online life stemmed from social platforms being designed specifically for viral "content" and designed terribly for actual conversation between humans. I was always chasing that next big "hit." The connections I made felt extremely shallow over time because so many people were liking or commenting or leaving me a fire emoji, but I was lacking deeper connection. I had eyeballs seeing what I was doing, but I felt no one was really seeing me. Twitter would reward my opinionated, attention-seeking tweets, but I was missing real conversation. I missed the actual, real pub-like conversation I was having when the internet was in its infancy—on the Facebook "wall" or in my MySpace inbox. Yes, I was getting these conversations in real life still, but, as an introvert who enjoys long periods of time alone writing, I was craving an outlet online that allowed me to feel as though I was properly connecting with someone like-minded. The truth is, I don't like constantly socializing; the internet was exciting to me because I could connect virtually. But slower, deeper, more real chats wouldn't allow the platforms we use to make as much money. The platforms started changing; it was less about sending long messages back and forth and more about quick and easy interactions. As the platforms become less about meaningful conversation and more about outward appearance and "likes," it's as if we're trying to communicate through one of those cheap homemade contraptions you'd make as a kid: two paper cups and a long bit of string. *I am not hearing you properly.* What we are trying to say gets muffled and misinterpreted, and it becomes frustrating to listen to it for too long. So we give up, or we tell the other person they are talking nonsense. In short: My online life and offline life were majorly clashing, and something needed to change.

It's important to be able to speak at length—or at least in proper sentences without being capped—to have room for nuance. Social media character limits and shareability are a recipe for disaster, leading to things being constantly taken out of context. It's as though we are just constantly reducing ourselves into headlines and no one is bothering to read the full article we are trying to communicate. The reality of the world can't be presented in "snippets." We can't connect in snapshots. Our real-world experience is large and layered, deep and dense, and the internet clashes with this. Humans are complex, nuanced, and multifaceted. We change our minds, are awkward, contradict ourselves daily, and therefore can easily be misunderstood. Being misunderstood is one of the most upsetting emotions humans can have. The more we spend having half-conversations online, the more we are losing context with each other. The more we feel ashamed, cast out, and alone. A cycle on repeat.

I felt it was important to write a book about being human (and retaining that humanness) in an increasingly technological world. As Simon Sinek says, "the human animal is a legacy machine living in a modern world—our brains are ancient machines trying to keep up. We still need people and connection to survive, the same as when we lived in caves and huts."[4] I wanted to write a book about how we can be better to ourselves and to each other. Plus, I—like many people reading this, I assume—

am pretty terrified and intrigued about what the next developments will be. Like the rapid advent of AI, for example. We all know it's coming and is already here, but it's happening behind the scenes, so we aren't fully aware of the larger-scale ramifications just yet. Our world is going to change considerably in our lifetimes—it's a matter of when, not if. Author Mo Gawdat, author of *Solve for Happy* and *Scary Smart*, told me, "Technology is magnifying who we are. [AI] is already much smarter than we are. In ten, fifteen years at most, it will be the smartest being on the planet." If machines are going to be "smarter" than us, then surely we will have no choice but to lean in to the things they don't have. Our humanity. Our creativity. Our real, deeper conversations. Our unique fingerprint on the world.

This isn't a digital detox book. Completely logging off and living in a hut to chant alone and meditate does sound quite nice, but I wonder how relatable or possible that is for the everyday person living their life. It reminds me of the episode of *Black Mirror* where the CEO of Smithereen (based, supposedly, on Twitter founder Jack Dorsey) lives like a monk in a rocky California desert—someone who has so much money he does a 180 turn to living a Buddhist life with nothing. I've read many older actors sniff at social media, calling it vulgar and unnecessary, but they don't mention that they happened to be lucky they entered the industry before they needed to be involved with it. Maybe you can log off completely. Maybe you have. Maybe you don't need the internet at all to do your job, or live your life, or see your friends. But most people are embedded now in the internet world, feeling it's worth it for the vast connection it gives us. This book is about people who want to analyze and control their future with their phone while also keeping a toe firmly dipped in. I want to lead my personal and work lives with technology embedded in both, but I also want to be reminded of hope, humanity, and heart. And I don't want to feel as though I'm being influenced twenty-four hours a day.

This book is for people who feel overwhelmed or engulfed by our fast-paced digital world. In it, you will find a series of practical prompts; so if you fancy writing as you go, make sure you have a pen and paper at hand. This book will suggest ways in which we can slow down, go back to basics, and avoid the temptation of "bigger, better, faster!"; how to decline the temptation to "scale" or "grow" absolutely everything you do, refuse to monetize every inch of your life, and bring more of a human feel to the internet again. There can be so much substance and growth in nurturing your online space. This book is for everyone. It's about being more human, and more ourselves, in a world that seems to be constantly interrupting and distracting us from that path. This book is about how we can enjoy the delights of the World Wide Web without being stuck in it like a trapped fly, connect more deeply with each other, and realize that we are enough. Target us all you want; we are already enough.

Emma Gannon, 2022

WHERE ARE WE NOW?

*"How dare you not cover the entire human
experience in a single tweet."*

—@laurenthehough

IN 2000, THE DAILY MAIL RAN THE HEADLINE: "INTERNET MAY JUST
be a passing fad as millions give up on it." Of course we snort
at this now, as though we were being told that oxygen is
just a crazy, soon-to-be-over trend that we soon won't need. I
remember an old boss at a magazine saying that social media
was just a "trend," that we didn't need to pay too much attention
to it—here today, gone tomorrow. Decades later, here we are,
practically injecting it into our veins. I don't need to remind you
of our COVID-19 lockdowns where we did *even more* from our
screens: working, socializing, attending events, taking quizzes,
consuming entertainment, shopping, seeing virtual doctors.
We could just about survive inside our four walls as long as we
had the internet. However, as we saw from lockdown life, "the
internet" is no longer something separate from us that lives

inside a box. It is now a huge part of overall "life." We should probably look more closely at what we actually use it for and how much time we feel comfortable being connected online. According to the online magazine *Inc.*, we tap, swipe, and click on our phones 2,617 times per day.[5] My eyesight has gotten worse recently from constantly staring at grainy pictures on screens. Right now, I'm being sold beauty products that have moved on from marketing messages about UV sunrays or harsh city pollution and on to blue light damage from our phones. The dreaded blue light. So, we can safely say the internet isn't a fad, but I think we are all privately brainstorming ways we can give up on it or have a better relationship with it—even just *slightly*. So how do we use it in a better, more intentional way?

PANIC STATIONS

Soon after hitting my thirtieth birthday, I hit "peak overwhelm." I needed to shut a few things down. I needed a smaller friendship group. I needed to just have *less buzzing* in my pocket. A box pops open on my screen: "Do you want to hibernate your LinkedIn account for six months?" Do I? It was almost as if they were double-checking I was sound of mind. *Are you sure you want to do this? Think of all those opportunities you might be missing out on!* But I click "Yes" and agree to my profile going dormant. I feel giddy and continue this buzz by taking another hit: deactivating my Facebook page. Upon deactivation, my profile picture immediately turns into a darkened silhouette.

I feel my shoulders drop. On my Google Pixel phone I click "Pause" on the Twitter app so it won't update or show me notifications until I manually click "Unpause." With all three of my main social media apps frozen, I feel so much lighter.

I knew I wasn't turning my back on them completely, but I felt like a person who'd had her head pushed under water and was now coming up for some much-needed air. I needed the reminder that I had a choice. Growing up as the internet evolved alongside me felt exciting for so long, but now suddenly here I was wanting it all to magically go away. It had become too much, and I had started to feel out of control. My relationship with it had suddenly changed. I was feeling let down by the original promise of it all: that we could use it to truly connect, and we could easily dip in and out. When we feel scared, we often go into fight-or-flight mode. But we don't need to completely flee. Let's use this moment to reflect on what we need and don't need and adjust accordingly.

PROMPT: What parts of your online life do you enjoy and do by choice (e.g., curating boards of inspiration on Pinterest), and what things do you do only because you feel you "should" (e.g., being on Twitter for professional purposes)? Unpick your "shoulds." Where are the "shoulds" coming from? You, your friends, society, your boss? Pinpoint who/what is making you feel like you should, and see if there's a way this can be addressed, tweaked, or changed.

YOU VS. ONLINE CULTURE

Harvard-trained sociologist and life coach Martha Beck says we have two selves, our "social self" and our "essential self." Our social self knows how to be polite in meetings, wear clean underwear, and eat our food with a knife and fork (in other words, the learned behaviors and social codes we adhere to), but our essential self is the one we must protect at all costs. Our wild, true self. The self that is full of love. That self is very special indeed—it's our very being, our true nature, the real us stripped away from culture, our childhood self, the self who lights up when we do certain things. During my twenties, I was being led mostly, if not solely, by my social self. My essential self was nowhere to be seen. My childhood self would dance freely in public and enjoyed wearing mismatched clothes. What music would she like? What clothes would she wear? What would she really *think* beyond what she was being led to think? What opinions would she have that weren't just echoing the people within her bubble? I stared at my phone— the thing that used to bring me so much joy, freedom, new information—and asked myself, What am I actually using this device for now? What is my mission? And how do I find myself again?

So many problems stem from feeling disconnected from ourselves. One of the worst feelings for any social animal is abandonment, and that is why it hurts so much when we abandon ourselves. When we abandon our true selves—our minds, our bodies, our problems—and push it all down with distraction, scrolling, and shutting off, we start feeling like a lost child. There is no one there for us if we aren't even there for ourselves. Ignored, unheard, confused. We start acting out of character. We are more likely to compare and despair. We are more likely to make impulse decisions. Our obsession with the online popularity contest and with feeding our online profiles means we are in danger of leaving another part of ourselves behind in favor of a quick "like" or a comment.

PROMPT: Plan a "nostalgia afternoon." Play old music from childhood, watch old films that you might have watched with grandparents, connect with an old friend over a coffee and talk about the past. What things, or parts of yourself, do you miss from that time? Is there anything that made you feel good that you've left behind, that you could incorporate into your life again?

HUMAN VS. MACHINE

Technology has definitely made us productive. It's definitely made me fast at work. We get more done, but we don't know when to stop. Like when vacuum cleaners were first invented, it didn't mean housewives chilled out more. They actually just cleaned more, and the standards of cleanliness increased. It's sad, really, just how much more we work now, and how society makes so many of us feel "lazy" even after doing a very long day's work. In the lead-up to writing this book, I was quite busy, and a few people around me commented, "You're a machine!" They meant it as a compliment; they were being nice—but it triggered me. I don't want to be a machine. I want to be a human, and I don't want to be praised for how much I can "pump out." The year of 2020, when I spent the most time on my laptop ever, made me feel like some sort of content farm, a production line that kept churning. But nothing blooms all year round. Human beings have ups and downs, whereas machines—with no capacity for emotion or need for rest—can carry on. To stay human in an online world, we have to rebel against this idea that we must optimize, monetize, and be as productive as machines at every twist and turn. Repeat after me: You are not a machine.

> **PROMPT:** Block out an hour per day in your planner just for you. It can be an hour early in the morning, your lunch break, or the hour before you go to bed. Put it in your planner as if it is an important meeting and fill this hour with something you want to do—not need to do but want to do—just for the fun of it. A machine wouldn't do this. How rebellious!

GOING ANALOG

I feel I've pushed myself so hard in terms of online productivity over the years that I am now going the other way. I use paper diaries, I write by hand when I can—it helps me slow down because I'm such a fast typist that my work output is scarily fast sometimes and my brain cannot actually catch up. It's why

Julia Cameron's "Morning Pages"[6] works so well for me—the act of writing by hand brings up such a different voice and feeling than tapping and typing away. We can't compete with machines, and we shouldn't need to. We can only work like humans, which is to own our human rhythms. Business author Tony Swartz writes in his books about managing our energy, not time, and explained on HuffPost.com, "Our bodies operate by the same 90-minute rhythm during the day. Researchers have called this our 'ultradian rhythm.'"[7] We should lean in to our natural energy spikes and normalize our need for rest. You could even say that leaning in to what makes us human is, in fact, the future of work. What is the point of acting more and more like robots in a world that will one day be populated with actual robots? Speaking with NPR, *New York Times* technology columnist Kevin Rose looks at this: "We have been preparing people for the future in exactly the wrong way. . . . What we should be teaching people is to be more like humans, to do the things that machines can't do."[8] Quite. Our softer skills, such as creativity and irrational human messiness are what will make us stand out in the future. It's never been so important to lean in to what makes us human. Our obsession with productivity might one day be meaningless anyway because we can't compete with machines. Maybe it's time to be more unproductive, take the longer way round, and lean in to that.

PROMPT: You don't need to optimize your rhythms if you don't want to. But if you want to do something with focus, leaning in to the ninety-minute rule is a good way to do it. Set yourself ninety minutes on the clock. Turn your phone on to airplane mode. Get a blank piece of paper and start writing a list of things you used to love doing as a kid or have enjoyed recently, a place you'd love to visit, images you can't stop thinking about, or big dreams that often feel "silly." If you have any magazines lying around, cut out any pictures you feel drawn to. This piece of paper is a signal of what you may want to move slowly toward or include more of in your life. See if your online feeds match the energy/themes of this piece of paper. Follow/unfollow as needed.

BEING MORE HUMAN WITH EACH OTHER

Connecting or reconnecting with someone is an act of vulnerability. Reaching out and not knowing quite what response you'll get back can be terrifying. Showing our face without a filter, showing a messy room in our house, or telling someone about our mental health can bring us so much closer. A phrase that I think about often is "the jig is up," something that author Glennon Doyle says. Finally, many of us are showing up as our real flawed selves, admitting that the performance we were putting on is now officially over. We constantly project, broadcast, curate, and "brand" things online—it's tempting to showcase a life that looks better than it is. I agree whole-heartedly with something that Jennifer Romolini said recently on Twitter: "I just want everyone to stop pretending—that they know more than they know, have done more than they've done, look younger/thinner/more symmetrical than they do. It's all the fronting that's exhausting, keeping us from seeing each other, a waste of our finite, precious time."

PROMPT: Ask yourself gently, What are you covering up? What is the one thing, or couple of things, that you are worried anyone would know about you? Try the "worst-case scenario" exercise. What would be the worst thing that could happen if someone knew this about you? Sometimes our heaviest thoughts can open a lock to some of our deepest relationships. We don't need to hold so many secrets.

WE ARE TIRED:
THE ERA OF INTERNET FATIGUE

HERE IS AN EXAMPLE OF HOW FATIGUED WE ARE: THERE IS A
Facebook group that exists where you pose a low-stakes question
and the members of the group make the decision for you. It says:
"Can't decide between two shirts? Can't choose between pizza
or spaghetti for dinner? Let this group make small decisions for
you."[9] It has 143,000 members. It reminds me of the monologue in
the second season of *Fleabag*, when Fleabag is in the confession
booth: "I want someone to tell me what to wear every morning.
I want someone to tell me what to eat. What to like, what to hate,
what to rage about, what to listen to, what band to like, what to
buy tickets for, what to joke about, what not to joke about. I want
someone to tell me what to believe in, who to vote for, who to love,
and how to tell them." Sounds extreme, perhaps, but I do think
it sums up a general feeling of being overwhelmed, of to-do lists,

decision fatigue, choice paralysis, of the growing number of apps on our phones and the growing number of pressures put on us. We have so many options available to us now that sometimes I do look to the internet to tell me what to do. When we have too many choices to make, they get into a bottleneck, and we become stuck.

Social media, and the way we are currently using it, is fatiguing us. Over time, it has become a very different place from the online world we entered decades ago. Of course, "the internet" or "social media" isn't its own separate solo being that we can blame everything on—it is simply a reflection of us, the collective people who use it. But the algorithms, gamification, and built-in technology have changed our behaviors, exhausted us, and, quite frankly, manipulated us in the process. We reach for our phones first thing in the morning. We scroll until our eyes hurt. We focus on pings and dings and likes. We are taught that having a blue verification is synonymous with social status and a life of perks. We are rewarded for reaching "inbox zero" as though it's the most difficult level of Candy Crush. Instagram is yelling self-help quotes at us—full of "you shoulds" and "you shouldn'ts"—telling us that if we are not resting enough, or working enough, or if we don't have a perfect work-life balance, then we are a failure. It wasn't that long ago when social media sites were a seemingly innocent place where we could talk to friends and express our identities through song lyrics and photos and "pokes"—but then we gorged and gorged. And now look at us. The bags under our eyes are practically suitcases now.

We are tired of being lied to, of companies creating tools and apps that they won't even use themselves. In 2017, a piece ran in the *Independent* newspaper about Justin Rosenstein—the man who invented the "like" button on Facebook—stating that he had in fact deleted the app from his phone. At the time he invented it, he believed it was "awesome" but later admitted he feared it brought "bright dings of pseudo-pleasure."[10] In 2020, Netflix aired the documentary *The Social Dilemma*, which at first I thought was just telling us everything we already knew. But it showed us, via the horse's mouth, how much darker it had become—resulting in the former employees at the big tech companies who designed the interface and engineered the addictive algorithms to come clean and cleanse their consciences. They explained exactly how the business models of social media companies are built on clever and strategic manipulation. They are now running for the hills, and some are setting up their "do-good" initiatives. Many believe that these companies first set out to do good (I'm not quite so sure), and it was suggested that the "like" button was originally intended to spread positivity throughout the world. (However, it did always feel weird to "like" a friend's sad news—because there was never any "dislike" button—and pressing a button is not the same as actually speaking to someone to check they're OK.) The "like" button has consequently been deemed one of the most "toxic" elements of social media by the Royal Society for Public Health, as users felt it would continually pull them back onto the sites through endless, pointless notifications. Interestingly, Instagram has since begun trialing not showing the number of likes a photo has. I have been experimenting with hiding the likes on my photos, and I'm loving it because it removes any measurement of a post's "worth" that was solely based on other people's decision whether to like it or not. The way we started to inherently think "Should I post this?" because we're trying to second-guess if people will "like" it is completely at odds with any creative output. Good riddance, "like" button. Of course, the person doing the posting can still compare/despair about how the post is "performing" even if no one else can see. It still sucks us into putting an arbitrary value or worth on the outward reception of our special life moments. I hope over time we can start to distance ourselves and unpick our relationship with this digital validation that most of us have grown up with.

When these platforms eventually sold their soul to advertisers, we—the users—became the product. We are not only being sold to but *being sold*. As compelling as the documentary *The Social Dilemma* is, it gives us a wake-up call but no real solution or next steps.

Why are we so desperate to cling onto social media? What's the fear about stepping back from it? I often wonder if it's to do with the sunken cost fallacy—that we are worried that if we step back now, we might have to face the possibility that we could have wasted a huge portion of our lives on it. So, we keep pedaling, trying to make it work for us. Our cultural obsession with productivity has also been exacerbated by our access to evolving technology—and perhaps we are now in so deep that we feel as though we wouldn't know how to function without it.

There were lots of strange conversations that came out of spring 2020, when the whole world was told to work from home for a period of time. We were discussing Zoom fatigue, micro-managing bosses, and wearing pajamas on our lower halves. But one thing that really stood out was a conversation with a friend who was feeling down in the dumps about being reduced to just the basic mechanics of being online: typing, Zooming, emailing, churning, sending. She was missing the human contact, the brainstorms, the office chat, the handshake, the body language, the smiles. In short, she was missing feeling like a human. She said she felt like a robot, a machine, a thing that just presses buttons all day. And I said something similar. I felt like a "content farm"—someone who just posted things all day long on the internet. And regardless of your job, isn't that most of us now? Haven't we all, in some ways, turned into content farms? We've morphed into people staring into screens, whether that's creating content for a living or sending emails at work or posting your family photos on Facebook.

We are also fatigued by the amount of online abuse—especially that which is targeted toward women, and specifically toward women of color and the trans community. You wouldn't go to a pub where people were shouting and threatening to kill you, so why would you want to hang out somewhere like that online?

We are living in a time when, sadly, many people who feel threatened by someone else's differing beliefs can turn into online trolls. As Steve Almond said on *The One You Feed* podcast, "One of the basic forms of convenience now is the convenience of not having to see people you disagree with politically or socially or otherwise as fully human." This is the huge issue—people not seeing other people as human and therefore thinking they can spout whatever hatred they want to them. It's still an issue that doesn't have enough support or resources surrounding it. We can call the police if someone is being hurt, attacked, or abused in the street, but online we just click a "report" button that doesn't really do anything. Why hasn't this evolved? Why hasn't this been taken more seriously? I'll explore this later in the book when I discuss how to be a better online citizen.

We are fatigued at feeling as though we have to play a game to be seen. This applies in our personal and professional lives. It's not healthy for our lives to be performed and ranked. A friend recently made a joke that his baby announcement and scanned photo had a "high level of engagement." When you really think about it, it's so weird that we are currently living in an online world like this that has been engineered for some posts to "perform" better than others. It harms our relationship with our work too—for artists, creatives, and business owners, for example—when we start second-guessing what we should write, post, or share.

It's time to reconnect with ourselves, our most basic childhood selves, who were creative, direct, and exploratory, and who believed in basic fairness. When children see unfairness, they call it out. When children want something, they go after it—even if it was a delicious piece of cake, a big fluffy toy, or a yellow plastic spoon. If we could only be more like that, we would find a way, we wouldn't be so influenced, we would want to express ourselves fully in our own way.

A TRIP DOWN MEMORY LANE:
THE NOUGHTIES TO NOW

I CAN STILL VIVIDLY REMEMBER THE EXCITING BRIGHT LIGHTS OF the MySpace homepage. It felt like an arcade. One New Friend Request! Five New Messages! Two New Comments! One New Event Invitation! Ding ding ding. So many juicy and delicious morsels, stacked on top of each other. It felt like being a kid in a candy shop. A supermarket sweep, with a basket and countdown clock, not knowing where to start or what to gobble up first. Each clickable link was written in an urgent deep-red font with exclamation marks tempting you in, knowing that as soon as you clicked, you'd instantly want another. Because I had to wait until 6 p.m. to log in (cheaper landline costs back in the day), I would actually feel the dopamine rush as I hit "refresh," like a big swoosh over my whole body, as if I'd hooked it into my veins. My eyes would widen, the reflection of the late-night computer screen twinkling in the middle of my large pupils. ("The Glaze," I now call it—when you fall into a scroll hole like your mind has been hijacked; I still have to watch out for it. I don't want to be one of those couples who sit in silence in restaurants just scrolling, scrolling.) I remember being livid that I had to share the computer with the rest of my family, that I only got an hour to feast. I wanted to be deep inside the internet world. I wanted to stay there. I wanted to climb inside. (Little did I know that would actually be an option later in life—a hideous option—to be online 24/7.)

Between endless pings of MSN friends and the *Sims* "cheat" password, I was in heaven for most of my teen years because of this new, exciting world. It felt new because it was—the internet had only been around for a couple of decades. A privilege to have a computer in the home. The online world at that age felt more exciting than school, the playground, even books. It was a world of fantasy and opportunity. An endless roulette of chat rooms, games, and the excitement of boys saying "hello" to you first. Now, I'm trying to look back at this time objectively. Did I enjoy it as much as I thought? Was it, deep down, my choice to spend so many hours in front of a screen? How long did I spend doing things that were useful to me vs. making the platforms money and giving me nothing? Was it free will, or was I taken in by the razzle-dazzle of websites created by digital scientists who consider you a mere lab rat, who see dollar signs in your glazed-over eyeballs?

When people make assumptions about the differences between millennials and Gen Z, people assume millennials "had a real childhood." By that, they mean mostly offline, with muddy shoes and scraped knees. Yes, we climbed trees and weren't constantly plugged in, but the notifications were constantly on my mind even then. Once I'd tasted it, I wanted more. Whenever my friends and I hung out, we would gather around the computer. It was an activity, a sport. We were getting good at building our internet selves before we knew what "personal branding" was. We were teaching ourselves to "research" (stalk) people from the year above or below, fancying ourselves as mini detectives because people hadn't quite learned what "putting your account on private" meant yet. Exhibit A: the excruciatingly public "Facebook Wall." But is it fair to call an offline childhood a "real one" and a digital childhood "a wasted one"? We normalize and justify our internet usage every day. It's fine. It's just the way we live now. We don't worry too much when we see children hooking themselves into their digital devices, propping up their giant iPads in front of their dinner, wearing huge headphones, exiting the real world, and entering a virtual one. It's the new TV. We don't worry too much that we're all looking down all the time on public transport, necks curved like hungry giraffes. We don't think anything of "The Glaze." We don't worry that our souls are being vacuumed up and spat out as pixels. This is just life! This is how we want to spend our time! We're all sucked in while the Silicon Valley techies don't want their own kids using the tech they built. I keep thinking about what Zadie Smith said in 2019 on the *Literary Friction* podcast about the evolution of our technological world: "You are told day and night it's inevitable, and this is just how it is. It starts small, and then the amount of things you hand over to the technology gets larger and larger. . . . The exchange was always convenience. Very convenient with the [Google] Map and everything. Can't deny that. Bloody useful to have a map. The despair comes from—in any political system—when you feel you have no choice."[11] Zadie explains, beautifully, that there is a fear of feeling like our freedom has been slowly, subtly taken away. When you reach for your phone first thing in the morning, before perhaps thinking about your partner, family, self—is that freedom? Because it is starting to very much look like what it is: digital shackles. An invisible glue, bonding us to our tech. *I just want to feel as though I have a choice. I do, don't I?*

In 2007, it was totally normal to upload three hundred blurry pictures from a nondescript, uneventful night out, including the back of someone's head. Now, we painstakingly curate our feeds, picking the one filtered photo that we believe truly reflects us, expresses us but will more importantly "engage" our "followers" and work well with the app's algorithm. So much has changed, but at the same time, nothing has. We've always been online, always hunting out the next notification. But going into my thirties made me reflect on this in a whole new way.

Looking back, I used to assume my internet addiction grew gradually because the technology did. At fourteen, I would pay for a bundle of SMS messages (using them sparingly), log on to a slow computer at an internet café for a ten-minute session, or clutch a chunky phone that couldn't accept photo messages. I wasn't spending as much time on it, but I felt the same way toward these things as I do now, toward my speedy Google Pixel and MacBook Pro. I was hooked then, and I am hooked now. An innocent childish curiosity of buttons and codes and screens eventually turns into a day job full of buttons and codes and screens. The technology has changed and grown and sped up, but I still feel that same insatiable feeling as I did when I stared at the MySpace homepage.

But is it also possible that many of us are finally falling out of love with it?

Many friends of mine are leaving the internet. Twitter is full of goodbyes and declarations of a better life. The reasons for leaving are wide-ranging, not only because of the data-collecting, information-mining, or cookies (I suppose many of us have come to terms with that) but also mainly because it's become an unbearable place to hang out. Whether it's feeling bored of being constantly sold to, or told off, or told what to think, or the sight of aspirational people inviting you to watch tours of their million-dollar "forever homes" on the day your boiler packs up, or simply because it feels overwhelming, uncreative, or stale to have to think of something to post every day.

As much as the internet has made me great friends, built my career, given me opportunities to travel—all based on community and connection—real connection is what I want to focus on, talk about, and share resources on. I fear it's become lost among the bells and whistles and quick hits of dopamine.

MILLENNIALS ARE OLD NOW

"Pointless apps. An Is it dark out? app. A hold the button for as long as you can app. A put your mouth on the corner of your phone and tilt your head back so it looks like you're downing a beer app."
—Avery Erwin, "How I Fell Out of Love with the Internet"[12]

Born in 1989, I'm only a few years away from being what is now dubbed the "geriatric millennial." For those who aren't in reach of Urban Dictionary, this means an older millennial who is thought of as being young and cool but is actually pushing midthirties or even forty and is partial to wearing a pair of Crocs. Millennials might have grown up online, but now a lot of us have had enough. Getting the ick. (And it's not just millennials.) Everywhere I look, I see friends of mine taking a step back, either undertaking a mass unfollowing or just feeling as though they have reached some kind of mental "peak" with their internet consumption. We are so entrenched, in so deep, that we have genuinely forgotten how to switch off properly.

Maybe I look back too fondly on the early days of the internet. But it did feel exciting. When I asked on Instagram "What do you miss from five–ten years ago online?" these same themes kept appearing:

1. Authenticity. People felt they could express themselves more freely back in the day, and it felt less contrived and curated.
2. Less fear. People felt they could post private jokes without risk of being taken the wrong way
3. Blog communities. People genuinely connected over like-minded topics and making friends.
4. Spending less time online. People didn't feel as constantly tethered to it, because we didn't always log on via our phones (i.e., didn't have email on our phones yet). We weren't physically as addicted. We weren't using our thumbs as much!
5. Less advertising. We weren't being sold to every five minutes and therefore navigated the internet in a different way, perhaps for free.
6. Less urgency. We used to understand that the internet was a part of life but not the main thing running the show. The day emails went onto our phones was the day we moved from being slightly disconnected to being constantly "on."

The same type of answers came back when I asked, "What one thing would people get rid of or change today if they had a magic wand?"

1. Get rid of the ability to post hateful content. Bullying. Trolls. Revenge porn postings. Anything that harms another person.
2. Introduce tougher penalties for online abuse.
3. Eliminate intrusive advertising and companies that still do not respect the General Data Protection Regulation.
4. Reduce the ability to create/use bots.
5. Eliminate fake content, be it filters, fake news, or "deep fake" videos.
6. Removal of "likes" to end popularity contests.
7. Reduce the ability to swing elections or politics.
8. Take away anonymity and introduce an e-identity card.
9. Allow fewer notifications in general.
10. Make it easier to opt out of sharing any of your data.

Reading through the list, it's clear that the things we would like to remove are the main things getting in the way of what we want more of: real human connection, protection, and community, and a simpler way to access these things.

MUTE KEY WORD: ~~INFLUENCER~~

*"Social media has really altered our perception
of where we should be in life, what kind of
person we should be with, who we should
befriend, what we should own, how we
should feel about ourselves/others."*

—@viasimone_

I HAVE JUST RECEIVED AN EMAIL FROM BILL, WHO CLAIMS HE CAN
buy me "REAL" followers for a few hundred dollars. He states
they are "ORGANIC REAL & ACTIVE FOLLOWERS from Ads."
I have no idea what this means. He is selling Instagram video
post views for as little as sixty dollars for 50,000 views, and for
a million views it's $349. Pretty cheap, to be honest! Oh, and he
is also offering an Instagram verification service—for a special
price, you can get that coveted blue verification. I am grossed
out but also intrigued. Who buys this stuff? Who feels good
about building a castle made of sand? Who is real and who is
fake on Instagram these days? There are a few obvious clues to

how to spot a phony online, but I think the smoke and mirrors are growing by the day. I shudder and obviously delete the email. I have spent the best part of ten years building a relatively strong medium-sized social following. In a world of dishonest hares, I am happy to be a slow tortoise.

Of course, as with everything, there are two sides to the story, and influencers can also be a force for good. Instagram can be a place of inspiration, creativity, and community. Writer and creator Megan Jayne Crabbe (@meganjaynecrabbe) has tangibly helped me love and shake my body more often; activists like Gina Martin have shown that just one person can make a huge difference and even change a law; and writers like Nova Reid have influenced me to go deeper into unpicking biases so entrenched that, dangerously, I didn't even know they were there. If "influencer" is just a word for "people who influence others," there are hundreds and hundreds of people doing good work in that area. Plus, I'd rather have the choice of following a variety of influencers and online channels than only having a handful of TV channels, radio, and newspapers at our disposal; crazy to think it is all we had for so long.

IT'S NOT ALL ABOUT NUMBERS

I think it's the biggest myth that followers equal value or status. It is a dangerous myth because it breeds an environment and culture that focus on vanity, metrics, and competitiveness. Like everyone, I got sucked into this narrative, that if I "had enough followers," I would get the career of my dreams. It doesn't work that way. In fact, meaningful connections, genuine networking, putting out things you feel good about, and memorable conversations are the things that lead to fulfilling opportunities—and feel much better too. I know plenty of people running six-figure successful business with no more than three hundred followers (i.e., clients or prospective clients) following them. Having loads of followers is a very hollow goal; if there is not a solid foundation or reason behind the platform serving people and having a purpose, it can easily lead to feelings of emptiness.

As artist and activist Rachel Cargle said on Instagram: "I know in the age of social media it can seem like you need a 'platform' to do meaningful work. To influence now has an irrational prerequisite of a 'k' existing behind your follower count. Not true in the least. Your home is your platform, your extended family is your platform, your office is your platform, the little girl in your neighborhood is your platform, your classroom is your platform, your example of being a thoughtful person who cares about humanity and demands justice is. your. platform."[13] We all have a platform, we all have a voice, and we absolutely *all* have influence.

The word "influencer" doesn't just mean someone with mountains of followers. Everyone influences other people. Even if you have three people following you, and you post a picture of a restaurant you love, and one of them follows suit, you have influenced someone. If we are #influenced, that's because we actively engaged with whatever the message was. We have an active part to play. We are complicit in what we follow and engage with. The world "influencer" seems to have lost its meaning.

WE HAVE A CHOICE

We don't have to follow anything we don't want to. Some influencers post about stuff that most people cannot afford (and neither can the influencers most of the time; they get it for free), but it's the same as choosing to buy or not buy *Vogue* magazine. There is something out there for everyone. I don't follow influencers on private jets, just as I don't buy interior magazines that are out of my price range. We don't have to follow it—or we can follow it for some "aspiration," which can be fun too. We get to choose. That's the beauty of it.

EVERY HUMAN WANTS TO FEEL SEEN

We think we want followers, but we actually just want to be seen. We're human. We want to be understood, and unfortunately, because of the two-dimensional way the internet works, we end up feeling misunderstood a lot of the time. People can read into our captions the wrong way, they can make assumptions about our situation, they can fill in the gaps that have been left unfilled. How can we be properly "seen" through a narrative that we have made according to what we think people want for us? How can we feel "seen" when we are open to feedback from people we don't know, who don't know what's best for us? Entrepreneur Cathy Heller said something interesting on my *Ctrl Alt Delete* podcast when I asked why so many of us want to be seen in this way, by having followers or having our name in lights: "Every human wants to feel seen, and we want significance. That's good, that's not a bad thing, we want to come to this earth and know that it mattered that we were here. However, the way that we get that is from the actual transaction of meeting another human being and contributing to them and feeling like you made a stamp, you made an impact, you made an imprint." That deep feeling of connection doesn't come from broadcasting your life to people or only showing the shiny bits. Sometimes, however, I think we get confused between wanting to be seen and wanting social significance, wanting followers, wanting a new thing, or wanting online validation and likes. Of course, we would get these two things confused. We can feel "seen" in other ways.

AN INFLUENCER OR A BOT?

When I first worked in social media, a so-called influencer was a rare breed—the new celebrity, someone online with something to say. An influencer was an everyday person who had used the internet to garner a following and eyeballs (be it conversations, recommendations, education, or reviewing their favorite Primark items), and the eyeballs turned rather quickly into money. Cut to 2020, the global influencer marketing industry is currently estimated to be worth $5.5 billion and predicted to grow to $22.3 billion by 2024, according to research by Markets and Markets in 2019.[14] Big money.

I don't have an issue with this. I also sometimes make money in this way by collaborating with brands that I gel with and am maybe classed as an "influencer" in certain collaborations. As the cool kids say, "Secure the bag." Take advantage of a new industry and take the money that corporations are willing to pay for your work and spread your message.

However. It's all very well if someone has nurtured an internet space through organic means. But a study undertaken by Swedish company A Good Company saw that as the influencer industry is growing, so is fraud. *PR Week* estimated "wastage" costs the industry close to $750 million globally.[15] In other words, many people are just shouting into the void or speaking to bots. People have become so obsessed with followers that they don't even care if they are speaking to real people anymore.

The reason we get annoyed when we get put "on hold" or put through to an automated voice is because we want to speak to an actual person. We don't want a robot asking us to press buttons. It's one of the most frustrating things that we all have to do sometimes, and we hate doing it. I feel the same frustration when I see people using fake bots to grow a brand online. The internet should be full of actual people, not automated people.

I have an email folder where I save strange emails from niche agencies. From a quick scan I can count multiple ways they are breaking GDPR rules, offering me ways in which I can "enter a competition" and "win a database of email addresses and followers." I block automatic accounts that keep desperately asking for a "follow back." I notice when someone has bots liking their photos. It's hard to tell when something starts off with fake followers (though there are now agencies that can report on the "quality" or realness of a following) because, as social animals, when we see someone has lots of followers, we follow. Therefore, what starts off as fake can quickly turn into something real, and your average person would never know. This means we are blurring what feels true and organic versus something socially constructed. It makes me feel on edge. It's like suddenly not being able to tell the difference between a natural beach and a man-made one.

As I sit at home tutting, I also have genuine concerns that this minority of scammers threatens to ruin an industry that should be based on trust and transparency. And if it goes on much longer, I feel the bubble will burst. I think we need to go back to basics and concentrate on interactions over vanity metrics. I want to encourage stripping it all back again and reminding ourselves why building communities online is joyful and authentic. About why numbers should never be the goal, and that there are lots of examples of people and businesses thriving in different ways, people and companies that value conversation and customer service over and above social media followers.

THE ORIGINAL INFLUENCERS

I rewatched the nineties film *Wayne's World* recently. Thirty years ago (what?) Wayne and Garth came bouncing onto our screens as the original influencers; essentially a pair of YouTubers before their time, they tread that tricky line between making creative content and making a living. Product placement is nothing new. Even as early as 1927, in the Oscar-winning film *Wings*, starring the iconic Clara Bow, there was a not-so-subtly placed Hershey's chocolate bar in a scene. Human beings have always been sold to via entertainment. Underneath literally everything lurks a sales pitch. Even activism, feminism, and body positivity are commodities now. Everything can be placed on a T-shirt with a price tag.

The modern-day equivalent of this, of course, is the nonstop shop of social media and specifically individual online influencers. It's no different except now it's girls (and boys) next door who have amassed huge followings, and more traditional celebrities have the opportunity through apps like Instagram to have their own space to speak directly to fans—and can shape their own narrative outside of creepy newspapers like the *Daily Mail*.

According to *Forbes*, 84 percent of millennials stated that they did not like traditional marketing and 58 percent still trust the recommendations of their favorite digital stars over and above anything else.[16] Influencer marketing is hugely effective. Personally, it often scares me how quickly I "swipe up" on Instagram and get my wallet out. Half of me loves the sophistication of the targeted advertising (the algorithm knows exactly what I like!), and half of me is worried about my current spending habits when it's so easy to click. Up until now, it's been a bit of a free-for-all. The Wild West of online marketing. Luckily, the Competition and Markets Authority (CMA) has now clamped down on wishy-washy behavior where celebrities and influencers don't make paid content clear, including free gifts and free trips. Now it's a case of abide by the rules or literally go to jail. The fact that the CMA and the Advertising Standards Authority (ASA) are finally showing more genuine concern shows the true power of the industry—more powerful than most people think.

The growth of the industry is rapid with no sign of slowing down. Sixty-seven percent of brands use Instagram for influencer marketing and 80 percent of brands say they've increased the amount of content they produce—just a couple of many intriguing statistics on the Influencer Marketing Hub. The influencer industry clearly isn't going anywhere. The same report says that the influencer industry will have grown to $13.8 billion in 2021.[17] Though, just like us, brands are not immune to accidentally or not accidentally attracting a fake following. It's interesting that the same percentage of brands using Instagram are also concerned about influencer fraud. If this is the new world of online content that we are going to live in, and if this is the next phase of the so-called information age, then we urgently need to feel more secure that we're not being lied to. Scamming is rife, with everyone having to be constantly on guard, which is not an enjoyable way to experience the internet. I don't think we can solely blame influencers for being the ones single-handedly changing the state of the industry. We have to take some accountability for what we pay attention to. What we follow, click on, and give our time to will only grow.

THE POWER OF THE UNFOLLOW

I got an email recently from a woman whose husband very sadly had died. "Straight after my husband first died, I got hooked on following people on Instagram that were keeping fit all the time, saying, get up early, get out! But I just couldn't do it, and slowly learned that I would just exercise, my way, and when I felt like it. So eventually, I unfollowed those accounts." Following things that only make us feel worse about ourselves is no way to live. It's so important to pinpoint the things that drag us down and make us feel like we are not enough. That doesn't mean unfollowing anyone whom we deem to be happy and successful; if someone communicates in a way that lights and lifts you up, great! If someone is making you feel less than, unfollow.

> **PROMPT:** Perhaps we need to get better at analyzing true authenticity. What criteria are important to you before engaging with someone or something online? We should think critically before just being absorbed into whatever is popular. Everyone is an influencer now, and we get to influence our own lives. Unfollow anyone who makes you feel inferior, guilty, shamed, jealous, or anxious, and don't give anyone access to yourself online who you wouldn't let into your life in person.

THE ART OF BEING YOURSELF

*"Coming on someone's Instagram page and telling
them you don't like their content and expect them
to change it for you, is like knocking on someone's
door and asking them to change their furniture."*

—@mcganroselane

WHO ARE YOU?

Being stuck inside for over a year during a pandemic does
strange things to your identity. Who are you if you are a gym
lover and your gym is closed, or a digital nomad without the
travel, or a chef without a restaurant, or a film geek without
the cinema? It's been tough on our psyches because so much
of our external life design feels like the very bones of who we
are. I wouldn't say I've had an identity crisis but more of an
identity cleanse. Most of the things I defined myself by have
evaporated into thin air. This has meant sitting with myself
more without the ability to needle these questions out with
people or seek the validation of people in my life. Like an

undressed mannequin in a shop window, bare for all to see. As the French philosopher Blaise Pascal famously said, "All of humanity's problems stem from (wo)man's* inability to sit quietly in a room alone."

In a work interview or on a podcast or at a dinner party, people often ask (in polite or impolite ways), *Who are you?* Or (the dreaded) *What do you do?* You take a breath, ready to explain who you are. You gather all the ways you can sum up the space in which you exist. We all have to do it, and it never feels comfortable. Self-promotion, in whatever form it takes, can be hard for all of us. "Selling" ourselves doesn't feel natural or human at the best of times. *Hi, I'm Emma. I'm a writer, a podcaster, a creator, a bookworm, a friend, a girlfriend, a sister, a daughter, a person doing stuff?*

Recently, I watched an interview with spiritual teacher Byron Katie, who was asked that exact question ahead of a Q&A. She was asked the standard question to kick things off: "For those who haven't heard of you, tell us who you are."

Except she didn't just reel off her bio. She didn't say, "I'm this and that . . ." based on her work and hobbies. Her response was not "the norm." I loved how she answered it. Instead, she said, "When you ask me to tell you who I am . . . just to play around a little . . . what difference would it make? Whatever I say or do, you're going to form a belief about me. You'll imagine

---

* I added the "(wo)."

who you believe me to be. So, who am I? Whatever you believe that to be is all I can be to you."

I found this so interesting. She was basically saying that it doesn't matter how you think you're coming across or how you *try* to come across; other people have already made up their minds about you. A reminder that we are almost powerless to control who we are to others. You can "define yourself" as much as you can, but other people will view you in whatever way they frame you in their own heads. If you are thought of negatively by a stranger, that's out of your control; just as if you are loved deeply by a family member, that's out of your control too. It's the decision they've made about you. What a freeing (and slightly frightening?) thought that we can't control how other people see us. That's why social media is quite jarring at times because it's an environment all about curating who you are and how you want to be seen.

When we're not physically together—as with most of 2020—we've been making all sorts of assumptions about each other. In our minds or over the internet, we've been imagining each other a lot of the time. We've literally been figments of each other's imagination simply existing in our silos.

To truly connect, we have to be our true selves, let go of the identity we've been clinging onto so hard, and let people look at us and just see us for who we are: people navigating through a changing world.

RECONNECTING WITH YOUR PHYSICAL SELF

I often reach for my phone as the easiest way to "relax," and I don't really want this to be the case. So, I schedule in activities each week whereby I cannot use my phone. This could be driving or getting a train to the nearest beach to swim in the sea or booking in a massage or going to the cinema. Of course, there are also free things, like meditating while putting my phone in another room, which for me takes slightly more discipline. I monitor how I feel now when I scroll: Is my heart rate up? Are my eyes glazing over? Do I feel irritable? Am I in a comfortable position? It helps me to rectify my behavior when I remember to tune into my body rather than completely zoning out.

> **QUICK PROMPT:** What activity could you schedule this week/month where you won't be able to be on your phone much?

SELF-CARE VS. NUMBING OUT

Lisa Feldman Barrett explains that we all have a "body budget." Every decision we make, everything we do, every action we take drains our body budget. We only have a certain level of bandwidth to give the world every day. And if we keep draining our body budget without replenishing, we get burned out. If we drink too much, stress ourselves out constantly, lack nutrition or sleep, we are draining our body budget more quickly than someone who is showing their body more love.

There is a difference between doing things that are restorative for ourselves (e.g., self-care activities that refill our energy levels, spending time alone, having a bath) and numbing actives (e.g., doomscrolling on your phone, drinking through the weekdays, watching ten hours of Netflix). It's a useful exercise to really look at the way you spend your "downtime" and be honest with yourself about how much is truly nurturing you and how much is just you wanting to numb out. There is nothing wrong with numbing out occasionally, but it can be helpful to really unpick why you are wanting to do it in the first place.

QUICK PROMPT: I used to think sleeping was "resting" (Box checked! I'm resting!), but we also need to rest with our eyes open during waking hours! What thirty-minute self-care activity can you schedule in before bedtime?

REFLECTING ON YOUR E-PERSONALITY

I have a friend who is completely different online and offline. People reading this may think the same about me. It's funny how someone can come across as a totally different person. She would pick fights on Twitter, roll her eyes, and just appear quite blunt to most people who followed her. In person, she wasn't like this at all! Warm, charismatic, constantly laughing, it was as though social media allowed her an outlet for a specific part of her personality. In the book *Virtually You*, the author Elias Aboujaoude believes part of the danger of such frequent internet use lies in "how the Internet allows us to act with exaggerated confidence, sexiness, and charisma." Nothing majorly wrong with that, but Aboujaoude calls our virtual self our "e-personality" and shows how it manifests itself in many different ways: from dating to every email we send and Facebook "friend" we make. We might indeed "prefer" our online selves—the filtered, controlled avatar version of us—but he makes the case that our e-personalities "seep offline" too, making us "impatient, unfocused, and urge-driven, even after we log off." Like when we interrupt perfectly lovely moments to take a photo because it's so engrained to do so, thus not being "in the moment" very often. There is also the argument that your online self could be more in tune with your *real* self and true nature. We can compartmentalize ourselves if we want to, but for most of us, living separate "lives" online and offline is no longer an option, either logistically or for our mental health.

QUICK PROMPT: What aspects of your e-personality do you like/dislike? For example, I like that I'm more confident online to join in on conversations, and I dislike how impatient the digital world can make me.

PERFORMANCE CULTURE

In my previous book *The Multi-Hyphen Life*, I write about the power of personal branding and self-promotion and suggest how to tell people about yourself and your work in a way that makes you feel natural and at ease without "the ick." It is a strategic business move, to brand yourself, the individual who is running your business. Even though building a personal brand is still valuable, it's important it doesn't cross too much into just "success theater" as author Lodro Rinzler calls it. I have definitely fallen into this trap, where I play out successful moments as though I'm onstage. It doesn't feel real; it feels like a performance. We also live in announcement culture—the incessant need to announce everything in a dramatic way. "So . . . some professional news!!" Entrepreneur Grace Beverley describes announcement culture as "our ever-growing need to announce everything we're doing, therefore perpetuating our anxiety of having 'things' to announce in the first place. This includes working towards 'announceable' goals and judging our success and that of others on the quantity (rather than the quality) of announcements made." We act as though the announcement itself is as important, if not more important, than the very thing we're announcing!

QUICK PROMPT: Is there anything you're working on currently that is more about the "announcement" or photo opportunities than the thing itself? Be honest.

GOING PRIVATE

According to *WIRED*, "we will see more people leave public platforms entirely, sticking instead to small communities and friendship groups on more private platforms like WhatsApp, closed members-only Facebook groups, Telegram, or Signal."[18, 19] It does seem to be that people are craving to go back to basics a little. I have a friend who is well known, and she has a lot of people who follow her on the internet. A few years ago, she started a private, separate Instagram account with a few hundred people on there. I felt honored to have this window into her life—not just her public life, which any Tom, Dick, or Harry on the internet could "follow." It was fascinating to see the very clear distinction between her public and private self. Her public self was including "swipe up" links to new fancy projects, hi-res images of her in expensive dresses, while her personal account was showing her raw behind-the-scenes self. She had been in and out of surgery. She posted about her scars. I feel so deeply connected to her, watching her vulnerable moments, that I wanted to reach through the screen and give her a ginormous hug. We *can* use social media for real connection, but that is harder and harder to do when we have masses of people following our every move. We water ourselves down. There is an irony here, that your "authenticity" can be the very reason you gain a massive number of followers, but once there is a following, you can no longer reveal your true authentic self because of too much exposure and you reduce it all down. I asked on Twitter whether anyone had a private personal account. Lots of people said they did to share pictures of their kids. Someone else said, "I keep it as my private photo album and take so much enjoyment out of getting 0 likes." I enjoy having two Instagram accounts for this same reason. I feel more *connected* by getting three likes from three members of my family than a thousand likes from strangers. Perhaps I get more of a sense of egoic validation from the thousands of likes, yes, but I don't feel connected. It's important to know the difference, I think.

QUICK PROMPT: Would you consider having a private account, just for a few close friends? Would you share things differently?

TIME: OUR REALEST CURRENCY

"There are just not enough hours in the day," we say, as our screen time keeps increasing. I remember an author once saying that someone had complained on her Facebook page of never having any time to start writing her novel. The author kindly mentioned that the writer had just written a five-hundred-word comment to her on Facebook so did have *some* time, let's be honest. The commenter just perhaps hadn't noticed that time spent on social media *could* be spent somewhere else. It's important to take some responsibility for how we spend our time. Meditation teacher Tara Brach says in her book *Trusting the Gold* that even when she had no time with a demanding newborn baby, she would sit on the end of her bed and meditate for three minutes. And just those three minutes made a huge difference.

QUICK PROMPT: How could you spend your time differently, even just three minutes? Set a timer for three minutes and write, dance, draw, meditate. Realize that even the shortest space of time can be filled with something meaningful, even when you feel you have no time.

ONE SELF, MULTIFACETED

It's draining to pretend to be something we're not or to be seen incorrectly. "It's impossible to present as anything other than a 2-D projection of yourself. So keeping up an appearance that in reality captures so little of who any of us really are takes a lot of emotional/psychological effort," says journalist Lauren Brown. One of the most treasured human experiences is to feel loved from all angles, *exactly* as you are, like Bridget Jones and Mr. Darcy. Whether that's having a good day, being sick in bed, crying with anger, or celebrating a promotion, only a few people actually see all the different highs and lows of one person—and this is what it means to be seen. On social media, it is impossible to show everything and all angles. Even if you livestream your entire life, it's not the same through a screen.

We have so many different selves. It does not make you automatically "more authentic" if you post a picture of yourself crying. You could be just as authentic having an extremely average day or a really good day. Being authentic is showing things as they are and being yourself as you feel in that specific moment. On *Poets & Writers*, author Alexander Chee explains a breakthrough he had via his therapist, who said, "You are different with different people because you are uncertain whether you can be whole with any of them, and the result is that you feel inauthentic with all of them and you may even feel inauthentic *to* them. So, you need to pursue a complexity in the relationships you want to be your core relationships and that will help you feel more authentic to yourself." Talk about a mic drop. I reread this quote so many times and realize to a certain extent perhaps we all do this. We can be different with so many people, but our true self is layered and complex. Our social media presence is only one side of us. For years I didn't want the real "me" exposed on the internet. It was the perfect place to hide behind edited words and filtered images. Now, I am realizing how psychologically exhausting it is for all of us to not be seen in our full 3-D technicolor.

> **QUICK PROMPT:** Are you very different with the many different people in your life? Of course, it's totally normal to be slightly different, but are there any ways in which you can integrate yourself more, to be more of a full "you" with all people in your life?

COMPASSION FOR OUR PAST (DIGITAL) SELVES

Every so often, Facebook shows me a "memory" of what I was doing ten or twelve years ago. When I read my "caption," I shudder. I am not saying anything downright offensive, thank god, but I am saying something I categorically would not say now. I'm glad that Facebook is only showing *me* the incriminatingly embarrassing captions or funny "jokes" I'm making. I would not want anyone else to see them. We live in an era where our digital footprints follow us, which we are aware of now but weren't back then. When I think of teenagers now, who use Snapchat and Instagram Stories and apps that have "disappearing features," I think, *Oh, you won't have any digital memories!* And then I think, *Maybe that's a good thing—we don't need to document absolutely everything.* But a part of me is grateful that I can see how far I've come, and how much I've changed through these throwback moments. We should normalize the feeling of looking back at our past selves and cringing. Of course, people need to be held to account if they did something terrible, but I think there needs to be a window of compassion too in most cases where someone has made a one-off mistake, allowing people to change and grow. In terms of our work, we will always think it could be better. But there's a different lens we can put on it. As author Adam Grant once said, "If you feel embarrassed when you look back at your prior work, don't be discouraged. Take it as a sign of growth. You've improved your skills or raised your standards. Satisfaction can cause stagnation. Dissatisfaction with the past can mark and motivate progress." I find this quote really inspiring, and it's the reason I write and publish my books, safe in the knowledge that I might look back one day and think it could be better. But that's only a good thing—a sign of growth.

> **QUICK PROMPT:** Do you cringe at your past self, and past digital memories? Can you take a few minutes to feel compassion for that person who was still learning?

DIFFERENT FACES

Being more human online means showing myself as I am. I am going to admit here that I did have a short lived relationship with FaceTune—ironically in my twenties, the time when I *least needed* FaceTune! It makes me very sad to look back at some photos of myself and not *even know* if it is my real face or not. Although I can tell because my face is rubbed out like an oil painting, shiny like an egg. It makes me very sad to have ruined so many photos, but it has also inspired me to call myself out when I am tempted to do it now (even though sometimes I really want to use just a little bit of the "Paris" filter on Instagram. I know anyone older might roll their eyes at this, but at thirty-two, I do feel like my face is changing quite rapidly). But to me, it feels important to reflect reality and reflect a body and face that has laughed, cried, and lived. I used to nitpick and criticize every inch of my body (growing up in the skinny-jean, size-zero nineties culture was *a lot*), but now my kind thirty-something self says, "You look lovely and squishy. Now get into that bathing suit and go for a swim."

QUICK PROMPT: Follow more people online who show their unfiltered faces, bodies, selves. It has a ripple effect.

"THE ALGORITHM"

Me: *I hate all these intrusive online algorithms ugh so creepy pls stop.*

Also me: *Oooh my Spotify Discover Weekly page really *knows* me!*

Sometimes I refer to "the algorithm" as if it's the Wizard in *The Wizard of Oz* or something—some sort of all-seeing eye that we have to go and see or prove ourselves to. The Yellow Brick Road being the many ways we try to get closer to online "success." As though I am losing myself to wanting to impress the algorithm and changing myself to suit its mold. Of course, it's not a *Thing* but a set of calculations.

The algorithm is the most powerful thing—it decides what the world sees, what gets pushed to the top of the agenda, and what gets the most eyeballs and focus. As Seth Godin recently said in a blog post, the people who work at Google and Amazon and hold the meetings aren't necessarily the ones who create the noise or decide what people see; it's the algorithm writers behind the scenes who do that. He calls the algorithm writers the "weather makers" and everyone else the "weatherpeople."

The algorithm shows us the things it thinks we want to see. I remember watching a video of Eli Pariser back in 2011 explaining how my Google results of the same search phrase will be wildly different from those of my friends. If I search for a hotel or holiday, I'll get served a different recommendation based on my online data. Do you find yourself shopping the same look as everyone else or being advertised the thing you mentioned in passing to your friend over dinner? Sometimes I feel as though I'm in one big advertising feedback loop. Culture, logos, colors, branding all seemed to merge into becoming the same. Built for the 'gram: with the millennial pink, the rise of the sans serif font, the hipster aesthetic.

The other problem with the algorithm is it seems to be inherently problematic and skews what is seen by the masses. It doesn't serve a mission of diversity. As Danielle Pender, founder of *Riposte* magazine, described Instagram in *MagCulture*: "It's basically a shopping app now where influencers who promote oversized beige outfits from Arket have hundreds of thousands of followers and people of color have their content shadow banned or deleted."[20]

It's interesting to know what "works" in terms of the algorithm, and then it's freeing to forget about it. I enjoyed this piece of advice from agency Handsome Frank on the Creative Lives in Progress website: "Stop trying to please the algorithm and get back to basics. Make art for art's sake, make art for people, but don't chase the likes. One of the most worrying side-effects of Instagram would be if artists change the way they work in order to try and increase their Insta-popularity. This would be a huge mistake. Stick to what you do, and keep doing what makes you unique. Remember, you want to stand out, not fit in."[21]

> **QUICK PROMPT:** If there's no real way of discovering a "hidden gem" online, then do more of it in real life. Go to an antique shop, browse music shops or secondhand book shops, take a different walking route, discover something completely by chance.

DISPLAYING OUR TREASURES

On a basic level, social media is really just about showing people the things we like, think, and believe. I remember hearing Dolly Alderton on her *Love Stories* podcast (the episode with Matt Haig) describe how our use of Instagram as a sort of primal way of showing our identity is not a new thing at all. She described a trip to Orkney when she went on a tour of a Neolithic village that was uncovered in the mid-1800s. She noticed that in some of the stone houses there was a fire pit, beds, and then a little ledge for people to place bones, shells, and leaves—to display things that represented them or their family. "I think sometimes we forget . . . that the inclination to show who you are, express who you are, what you like . . . that's an ancient instinct." Sharing stuff on Instagram isn't new; it's just the newest platform we have. The problem is, the popularity functions on Instagram have made us feel as though we need to feel validation and approval for the things we like and that our choices must be up for public consumption. When I asked technology writer Taylor Majewski, she said, "I feel like being your truer self on the internet was once welcomed and celebrated! I feel disillusioned with the internet and social media now because it's so conformist there are 'aesthetics' that rule social media platforms which in turn detract from reality, individuality, and discovery."

> **QUICK PROMPT:** Write a list of three interests you used to have or want to have in your life, and pick one. Take pleasure and pride in enjoying this interest outside of Instagram, without posting about it anywhere online. Keep it back, just for you for a while, and see how it feels.

THE ART OF NOTICING

Daydreaming is a very important part of my life. There was a time when I realized I wasn't doing it enough, if at all. In Rob Walker's book *The Art of Noticing*, he encourages us to find ways to tune out the world's noise and focus on different things. As if we are children playing "I Spy" in the car—what can we focus on, instead of phones, when going for a walk, for example? In Julia Cameron's book *The Listening Path*, she talks about the importance of listening—not just to each other but also to yourself. When you stay very quiet, what do you hear? What messages come to you? What have you been forgetting? What do you want to focus on?

> **QUICK PROMPT:** If you can, book yourself a long train journey and stare out of the window for the duration. Afterward, quickly write down the things that naturally came to you during the journey.

PRACTICAL PROMPTS: RECONNECTING WITH YOURSELF

"Social media flattens the spirit. . . . To be free of this flattening, each day, honor your depth and remember that social media is a two-dimension speck in the fullness of your multi-dimensional self."
—Mimi Zhu

A. Get back in touch with yourself. Take yourself somewhere on your own—a night away or just in a different room in your home. Sit on the floor or lie down for twenty-five minutes. No music, no background noise, no audio, just you alone with your thoughts. Scary, huh? This is something we rarely do in our day-to-day. What thoughts surface? What is troubling you? What do you wish for yourself? Take every emotion in and let it wash over you. Be truthful. Write it down somewhere so you can return to it. Writing it down allows us to contain it.

B. Marie Kondo your digital feeds. Does your feed spark joy? Cull anyone who makes you feel anxious, less than, judged, or unworthy. As writer Leyla Kazim recently said, "I've Marie Kondo'd my Insta. Unfollowed ~160 (was only following ~300)—if it doesn't make me smile inside, it's gone. Shouty food porn, impersonal travel curations, nonsense tat etc. replaced with nature, art, talent, stories, friends. Now I actually look forward to opening it." Look at the list of the people/things you culled. Time for some introspection. Why do these things make you feel this way? It's important to look inward too. Are you feeling unworthy or anxious for reasons that might be untrue?

C. Reflect on your e-personality. Grab a pen and write a list of emotions you feel when you post online. Are you feeling confident? Worried? Detached? Grandiose? Anxious? Think about any tweaks you could make to your online behavior so that it matches up with the person you want to be. Are you living for "announcements," likes, and virtual hearts?

D. Whom do you trust? Trust is a huge part of human relationships. That's why, historically, we have shaken hands—to show we don't have a weapon. The vulnerability in that moment builds connection. It's important to have a circle of people you really do trust. You won't be able to trust everyone you meet on the internet, just as you won't be able to trust everyone you meet in the street. Write down on a Post-it Note five people you can trust. If you have more, write more. Whenever you are questioning something, instead of asking strangers for advice, turn to these people first. If you want to, you could also write a list of people you actively know you don't trust.

E. Go analog. If you are craving more of that "stumbled upon" feeling, something you could experiment with and buy for yourself as a gift is a mystery box of books. There are subscription services—like Feminist Book Box or Books That Matter—that will send you a bunch of books at random.

F. Block "me" time in your planner. Create a small portion of each day that's just for you. It doesn't have to be meditation, but carve out some time, as little as fifteen minutes, just for you. Ground yourself in the present moment more often, realizing that any time spent on social media is catapulting you either into the past or the future—past, because you may be looking at someone else's activity, or future, because we often use social media to plan our next move or worry about the state of the world.

G. Ditch the word "authentic." Over the last few years we've become obsessed with "authentic," ironically making it very inauthentic to appear overly authentic. Like when someone says, "I'm real" and you might raise an eyebrow and think, *Are you really?* It's interesting, though, our well-meaning attempts to now be real with people. Author and mindset coach Susie Ramroop now posts disclaimers on her Instagram to let people know they're not seeing the full story (for example: "What you are about to see in no way reflects the mood of my last few months"). It is interesting that we have come to this point, of wanting to be transparent, to show some context to our highlight reel. Here's a thought, inspired by one of my favorite thinkers, Seth Godin: Try being consistent instead of being authentic. Trying to be authentic feels forced. Being consistent is just you being yourself without overthinking it.

H. Ask yourself, "What parts of myself am I performing?" Showing you're a good person isn't always the same as actually being a good person. Performing allyship doesn't automatically mean you're an ally. You don't need to tell everyone everything or prove your humanity—you can do it quietly and impactfully offline. Sometimes our human emotion is too complex to say something meaningful in the moment when a huge tragedy has happened or to know when you're still figuring out whom you want to vote for. Some things don't translate well in a tweet, and it's OK to notice those moments when you join in before researching anything or retweet something without reading it. It's OK to notice so that we can make better choices online and offline.

I. Find your weird. As Seth Godin always says, "If you cater to the normal, you will disappoint the weird. And as the world gets weirder, that's not the smartest strategy." This is why it's quite depressing when everyone plays to an algorithm on social media apps. The algorithm therefore ends up making everyone act more and more "the same." A bit like when everyone on the planet wore the same black-and-white polka-dot Zara dress. People end up posting similar things because it "works" with the algorithm, and it takes away our creativity and vulnerability. There is a community out there for everyone, whether you want a podcast on Harry Potter, a Facebook group about gardening, or a newsletter on stamp collecting. Express your own personal style of weird! You're more likely to find your true friends this way.

J. Opinions for opinions' sake? Some days, I give myself a day off from having an opinion. I have personally found that the more strong, unmovable opinions I have, the more miserable I am. Of course, I have opinions about what is good and bad in the world that probably won't change. But when it comes to having an opinion on literally every single news item each day? I find it overwhelming, and sometimes

I just settle into thinking "I don't know," or "I haven't decided yet." Sometimes it is tempting to try to be overly cynical or rude because the Twitter algorithm, for example, rewards this behavior. If you tweet something overly shocking, it's more likely to get retweeted or engaged with in some way. As Tom Chatfield says, "The least viral thing is to say 'I don't know.'" No one can be an expert in absolutely everything that happens. And that's OK; in fact, it's great—it's the beauty of life.

K. Show yourself. One key difference between the online space and the offline space is that we can be anonymous online. At the time of writing this book, there is a petition to make verified identification a requirement for opening a social media account. I'm sure people will have many different opinions on this, but I do think we should take accountability for what we say or do on the internet. Anonymity makes trolls braver, and it would be a good thing for that bravery to be taken away—for people to have to look in the mirror and see their own reflection for what it really is.

L. Look beyond the noise and "trends." When something "trends" online, it means everyone is looking at that. What we really should be doing more of is looking at the stuff that doesn't trend. When things "trend," they distract us. When something is made into clickbait (be it a headline or some Instagram therapy advice), it loses its nuance, and we should pause and step back first before inhaling what we see. We don't always need to pay attention to what everyone else is paying attention to. Hidden stories about climate change, social activism stories that need sharing, smaller news stories—these also need our attention. Clickbait tabloid culture tries to water things down, but as brand manager Hannah Ridyard says, "Ultimately, these platforms weren't built to channel human complexity and the nuances of current affairs, so it's jarring and slightly depressing to see a continual recycling of '3 ways to end world hunger' posts that are unlikely to end in real action." Let's look beneath the viral content at the real stories bubbling away underneath—they need attention too.

THE ART OF CONNECTION

"Believing we are separate selves is one of the deepest illusions and the source of our suffering."
—Tara Brach, *Trusting the Gold*

CONNECTING WITH OURSELVES

ON A LOOP

There does seem to be an irony in how plugged in we are and how disconnected we can quickly start to feel. In Alex Holmes's book *Time to Talk,* he says, "Our rising levels of screen-time these days—without real person-to-person interaction, eye contact, physical touch, and so on—could well be a contributing factor to many people's growing lack of emotional connection. . . . we could be stuck in a vicious circle with this: the more time we spend online, the more emotionally disconnected we feel; and the more emotionally disconnected we feel, the more time we spend on quick-fix digital connection through social media, Zoom calls, interactive gaming, etc. to distract ourselves from the unhappiness."

> **PROMPT:** Do you ever feel like you're in a loop of feeling so hyperconnected that you actually feel disconnected? Next time you feel disconnected, instead of going in for more of the endless scroll, why not take yourself out for a date? Inspired by Julia Cameron's "artist date," take yourself for a day out—a museum, a café, a bookshop—and reconnect with yourself and take in the strangers around you. Sometimes feeling connected to the real world again, outside our screens, can be just what we need.

SETTING BOUNDARIES

I am continually inspired by the boundaries other people set for themselves. I emailed someone recently and promptly received an "out of office" saying, "I am on a much-needed holiday, every email will be automatically deleted. Email me again when I'm back." Another example I saw recently was someone who'd set up an automated WhatsApp message to say they were taking a break and to not expect a reply. Both are great examples of boundaries: nonapologetic. As a recovering people pleaser, I am at the beginning of my boundaries journey, but I'm starting to lay the foundations.

PROMPT: Signpost your boundaries. In your professional Instagram bio, it might read that you don't check DMs every day. You might put "away" in your WhatsApp bio. You might set an "out of office" to say you're taking some time for yourself. Be honest in your communication. A way in which we stop expecting so much of each other is to become increasingly honest about how hard we find it to constantly keep up. We need to break the illusion that we're all OK with level-one urgent communication for nonurgent things.

WHAT ARE YOU "KEEPING UP" WITH?

Part of the problem is the endless temptation to scroll. There is a human inclination to "keep up with the Joneses" (or the Kardashians), but as author and online creator Megan Jayne Crabbe says, "Keeping up with your time line is not more important than keeping up with your well-being." What do we mean when we say "well-being"? For me, a big part of that is feeling genuinely in touch with others and myself. An honest, intimate phone call to a friend or family member will keep me lifted for days. Ten minutes doing a breathing exercise or looking out of the window at the birds with a cup of tea.

PROMPT: What would you do right now if you had absolutely nothing and no one to "keep up" with? What would you do today if FOMO didn't exist? Write a list. "Do" the list!

PUT "UNPLUG" IN THE PLANNER

When I chatted to Venetia La Manna for my *Ctrl Alt Delete* podcast, she told me all about her no-phone weekends: She has installed a landline phone and goes offline for the full forty-eight hours, telling friends and family about it so they can contact her for emergencies in other ways. She calls it "#Offline48" and said on Instagram, "Switching my phone off for another weekend with the aim to be as present as possible—We all know the feeling when someone is trying to chat to us and we're only half listening because our phone is in hand . . . Not during #Offline48."[22]

> **PROMPT:** Block out a period of time in your planner to be offline. Treat it as though you are going on vacation. Let everyone know, and have some worry-free time offline. What would you do with forty-eight hours of no-phone time?

ADMITTING IMPERFECTIONS

We slip up. We learn by making mistakes. We have all done something we regret or said the wrong thing or offended someone without meaning to. Of course, we need to make sure we learn and grow and don't make the same mistakes again. A lot of discriminatory behavior can come from outwardly "well-meaning" people, but that doesn't make it any less painful or problematic for the person on the receiving end. I think we have to own up to our own imperfections without just thinking everyone else is the problem. In a tweet, activist Munroe Bergdorf—someone I hugely admire and, in my eyes, always goes about things so logically and maturely—said, "I'm not perfect, neither are any of you, we all slip up, we're all guilty of participating in toxic online behaviors at some point. But we can begin to make a change at any point, remove ourselves from situations and be conscious of the fact that we are all HUMAN." In Pandora Sykes's book *How Do We Know We're Doing It Right?*, she writes, "It has got to the point where many people are scared to express their point of view in case they are publicly shamed for not staying within the 'package' of ideas ascribed to them. . . . it is less about being right and more about *not appearing wrong.*" We will get things wrong, a lot. It's OK, as long as we genuinely understand where we went wrong and apply the lessons to our lives and make things better. When we are compassionate with ourselves, we can be more compassionate to others.

PROMPT: Get better at not fearing to appear wrong. Get comfortable with saying "I don't know" or "I'm sorry I was wrong about that," in small ways on a daily basis. Befriend the ego.

CONNECTING WITH OTHERS

SERIOUSLY, WHAT'S THE URGENCY?

In a recent *Irish Examiner* column, author Caroline O'Donoghue wrote, "While we are very keen to tell people to get off social and advise them to spend less time on their phone, we are still holding them to an extremely high standard of personal correspondence. Emails, text messages, and most eternally demanding of all, WhatsApp."[23] It really is a jarring reality. We are telling people to digitally detox while also getting miffed if someone doesn't reply to a message for a while. We see a person has "two checkmarks" on WhatsApp, send an email, and get annoyed if someone hasn't replied for a few days. We need to start acting as though pauses in communication are normal. Unless something is genuinely urgent (like a situation where the world will crumble if you don't get a reply—I can't think of many, unless you're Joe Biden), we need to let people off the hook for not beings always on. As writer Tom Goodwin says, "I've turned off all notifications, I keep my phone on silent. But it still feels more like harassment than connection. Part of the issue is modern etiquette and expectations, the expectation of immediacy and access." Let's all try to live less urgently.

> **PROMPT:** How quickly do you reply to messages? Sometimes we get ourselves into the trap of always replying quickly and therefore disappointing someone if we take longer. Get into the habit of waiting a few days if you need to. Set a new normal for yourself and others.

THE PARANOIA OF THE "READ" MESSAGE

Technology and the various ways we can monitor people have added a layer to our worries, especially if we already suffer with anxiety. I recently had a friend write me a message, terrified that she had done something to upset me because I'd read her message and been online but not replied for a couple of days. We later chatted it out, and she was going through an anxious phase and I told her I understood—we've all been there. The made-up stories in our head can feel loud and true sometimes when our phones give us mixed messages.

PROMPT: Put more pauses into your daily life and actions. Incorporate "Le Pause"—from Pamela Druckerman's book *Bringing Up Bébé*, the idea that when a baby starts calling out or fussing, French parents pause for a few minutes before immediately rushing to them, to see if the baby can self-soothe and settle on their own. Incorporate more "Le Pause" into your social media habits. Normalize pausing before replying and communicate to friends and colleagues that this is how you prefer to operate.

"CANCELLATION" DOESN'T WORK

At this point, someone being "canceled" seems like nothing more than a PR machine to actually promote someone further. I remember first noticing the trend of YouTubers being "canceled" years ago when their name would be trending in a viral hashtag "#[Insert Name] IsOverParty." It was an online "party" telling the world that [insert name] was "over" for selling a piece of merchandise for a bit too much money. This person went on to get more video views, more money, more recognition. They were far from over; in fact, they were just getting started. "Canceling" someone online doesn't work. I think the phrase needs to go. If someone has done something culturally "bad," e.g., "said the wrong thing," we shouldn't be afraid of a conversation. We should feel we can approach that person in a way that helps them take some time out to go and reflect on why they have deeply upset people. On the other end of the spectrum, of course, when people break the law, abuse people, perpetuate hate speech, they should be banned, reprimanded, or face legal consequences. But that isn't "new"; we have always done that. But because we are now using hashtags to do it, and it can happen more quickly, we are pretending it's a new cultural moment each time something hits the news. I don't think it's healthy to use "cancellation" for someone on Twitter who worded something incorrectly in the same breath as someone like Harvey Weinstein who actually had his career "canceled" for very good reasons. The word has become too colloquially used across so many hugely different examples. Using extremely broad umbrella terms like this isn't exactly helpful; it doesn't move things forward.

PROMPT: Unless someone has done something deeply, unforgivably wrong and belongs in jail (an important caveat!), use flexible thinking to ask yourself if someone you consider "canceled" is beyond forgiveness for a small mistake. Be open-minded to how you too are fallible in your actions. Is it possible you could have made a similar mistake before? How would you like to be treated? Would you like to be given a second chance? When has someone allowed this for you in the past?

REACH OUT TO SOMEONE, JUST BECAUSE

We've all seen the worrying mental health figures. We all know someone personally (or how it feels personally) who will isolate themselves during a period of feeling depressed. We need to connect, not just by encouraging people to talk but also to make people understand that they have support. Sometimes it's not even talking at length—it's just knowing someone is there. On a more everyday note, I'd recently forgotten the power of knowing someone is thinking of you. A few months ago, I came home from one of those days where everything went wrong (train delays, coffee spilt, demanding emails). On the mat outside the door to my flat was an envelope, and inside was a postcard from someone I follow on Instagram who I have met a few times. She was moving between countries, and wrote me a handwritten note saying the woman on the front of the card reminded her of me and that she just wanted to say how lovely it was to connect while she had lived in the UK. From my own experience, it's the small acts of IRL positivity that can really help and are often more effective than reaching out quickly on social media.

> **PROMPT:** Why not reach out to five people you haven't spoken to for a while and give them a compliment or tell them what you value about them? Buy some notecards and send them to five friends you haven't spoken to in ages.

BEING MORE COMPASSIONATE

We all have trigger responses—that knee-jerk reaction to an image or something someone has said. This morning (while writing this) I saw a picture of a woman on Instagram standing by the sea on vacation in Italy looking completely relaxed when I was about to go and sit at my desk and cry about how overwhelmed I was feeling. In that moment, I could have fed my mind thoughts of how unfair things are, how I wished I was by the sea instead, how I'm sure that woman has had everything handed to her on a plate. Instead, I decided to feel compassion toward myself: *You're feeling stressed right now, but it will dissolve soon.* And compassion for her: *I don't know what she's going through too.* Sometimes, it's as simple as this: It's sometimes not a great idea to go on a visual-based social app when you're in a bad mood.

> **PROMPT:** In a moment of jealousy, sadness, or feeling "less than," make a gratitude list and write down ten things you like about yourself. You will be instantly pulled out of comparison, and focusing on yourself again.

CONNECTING WITH STRANGERS

JOYFUL SMALL CONNECTIONS

As much as social media can breed comparison and increase the gap between false narrative and reality, it's worth reminding ourselves that it does also bring us together. There are so many reasons to feel grateful for its existence. It's been used a great deal to help spread awareness of missing people, fundraising initiatives, and activism; raise money for emergency medical care; find missing pets; and spot the signs of when someone is in need of urgent help with their mental health. The funny thing is the joy we get from social media doesn't have to be "big." It can be as simple as joining in with a TV "tweetalong," tagging people who inspire you, or joining in with hashtag challenges (like the #joinin initiative that Sarah Millican started a few years ago, offering those feeling lonely and vulnerable around the Christmas holidays a chance to connect). During the pandemic, social media was instrumental in setting up and running initiatives such as Hack The Pandemic—the group used 3-D printing to make face coverings, mask clips, and other devices, which were distributed to essential workers for free. I enjoy getting notifications from apps such as Nextdoor to see how I can help in my local community and actually contribute physically—it doesn't have to be a huge thing: lending someone a tool they don't have or helping someone solve a local crime.

PROMPT: If you are feeling powerless or feeling the weight of the world, find a cause/charity/community and arrange to donate your time/money/skills. Every time you feel that helpless feeling, use it as a prompt to turn it into a small act of kindness instead.

THE POWER OF PODCASTS

When I asked online what makes people feel connected (to themselves and others at the same time), many people answered "podcasts." The opposite of the vacant scroll or a clickbait headline, a podcast can help us experience deep connection with audio—another human voice that feels as though it's speaking to just us. Listening to two friends having a laugh while we do our washing up or hearing someone tell an anecdote while we're in the bath. My favorite types of podcasts are those hosted by noncelebrity people talking about a topic they absolutely love geeking out about. There is a power in audio in general: voice notes, audiobooks, local radio. Hearing each other's voices is human and the closest thing we have to being in person with someone.

PROMPT: Pick an activity/hobby/interest that you love and search your favorite podcast platform for a podcast on that topic. For example, I usually listen to the same podcasts on rotation, but I did this exercise and realized I love going to the cinema and never listen to film podcasts. Then I discovered the *Films To Be Buried With* podcast, and it reminded me of so many movies I hadn't watched for years.

THE ART OF CONVERSATION

"When smart, committed people disagree about
the answer to a question, you've found a question
worth pursuing and a discussion worth having."
—Seth Godin

I JOKED ON TWITTER THAT TWEETING ANY RANDOM THING, LIKE
"dogs are cool I guess!" will be then turned into a political
statement and marker of your core socialized identity within
minutes. Someone jokingly said back, "OMG you're the anti-cat
hate lady!"

This is how ridiculous some social media platforms have
become when trying to have any sort of casual (or serious)
conversation. We're seeing immediate hard agreement or hard
disagreement with no real middle ground for nuance. One of my
favorite things in the whole world is juicy, in-depth, honest conversation. A dinner party of interesting people. As a child, I *hated*
small talk (and still do). When people offer feeble weather chat or
"So, are you going to have a baby?" questions—just reaching for
anything to fill a silence—I'd rather have the silence. My favorite

moments in life are made of deep conversations with friends and family where you think, *I will remember this conversation forever*, and those rare occasions when you sit next to a stranger and you have a mind-glowingly expansive conversation that in a small way changes you. I love conversations that make me think differently, make me curious, make me ask questions. As Rainer Maria Rilke says in *Letters to a Young Poet*, "Do not now seek the answers, which cannot be given you because you would not be able to live them. And the point is, to live everything. Live the questions now." Live the questions! For me, that is a life worth living.

There are platforms that embrace open conversation with a good energy. This is different from "anything can be said." That is when hate-speech territory can be allowed, and I hope we can all agree that there is a line on that. But a place like *Red Table Talk* (a roundtable show with Jada Pinkett Smith; the tagline is "3 generations. 1 table. no filter.") is an example of people wanting to actually discuss things, laying it all out. An issue is brought to the table, and they cleverly, curiously, powerfully unpick it. They create a safe space for people to bring their ideas to the table; even if there is major disagreement, there is respect.

IT'S NOT ABOUT AGREEING
BUT UNDERSTANDING

The elephant in the room is the fact that, most of the time, our disagreements are based in fear. We lash out at people we love because of fear, we are defensive because of fear, we make strange choices when we are fearful. We can immediately dislike something or someone often because we haven't dug deep enough to understand their point of view. Martin Luther King Jr., during his appearance at Cornell College in October 1962, said, "I am convinced that men hate each other because they fear each other. They fear each other because they don't know each other, and they don't know each other because they don't communicate with each other, and they don't communicate with each other because they are separated from each other."

LOSS OF CONTEXT

Human beings over time, especially over years of friendship, build up context with each other. I remember a friend of mine saying there were things she'd say to her friends over dinner that she knew would get her "canceled" online if she said them publicly. These thoughts weren't even that controversial or "wrong" in the grand scheme of things. She was merely commenting on how the loss of context or nuance might get her in trouble. Friends have history with you, they know you, they know you are a good person, they know your entire self and your core essence. But experimenting with bigger questions or thoughts in public, without context, would mean that people would, or could, get the wrong end of the stick. This is the issue with social media oftentimes—one sentence, one thought, one opinion can be taken in millions of different ways. Depending on who is reading it, it can be interpreted so differently, as if it were spoken in a totally different language.

DIFFERENT ANGLES

Media and digital content have changed and evolved. We used to get our information from the same channels (TV and radio) and now we don't (except for that rare occasion when we're all watching the same TV show at the same time, but when does that really ever happen?). But mostly we are all consuming different things—different articles, different newsletters, different podcasts. If lots of different information is going in, it's possible that we will clash more because we might be coming at something from different views, based on something we read, saw, or thought previously. Really, we should pause more often before immediately writing someone off as uninformed or "canceled"—maybe, just maybe, there's been a misunderstanding. It's worth finding out first, I think.

IT'S OK TO CONTRADICT YOURSELF SOMETIMES

One of the biggest traps of our digital age seems to be that we have to build some sort of personal brand and then set that in stone for all eternity. I'm *this type* of person. Forever. But I think we are so much more fluid than that, and thank god we have the ability to change our minds, change our lives, and take a different path. I think about this Malcolm Gladwell quote a lot: "That's your responsibility as a person, as a human being—to constantly be updating your positions on as many things as possible. And if you don't contradict yourself on a regular basis, then you're not thinking." Designer Fanny Vassilatos says, "Nowadays, everything feels so much more permanent, like it is written with an indelible marker and filed in that big cabinet with your name on it. The same big cabinet which is basically your identity in your work environment, your social environment, and your public environment. Everything now has to be 'on-brand' and it's like you can't make any bad moves." I completely agree—the toxic side of "branding" oneself means we're taking away our own freedom to change as often as we like. Trying to be "A Certain Type of Person on the Internet" is stopping us from truly connecting with others. We should feel able to shape-shift, change our minds, try new things. One of the ways to have better conversations and be less defensive is to sit with ourselves and question ourselves more often. I am a fan of thinker and author Ayishat Akanbi, who believes that our fear of being "canceled" is stopping us from exploring awkward or uncomfortable ground with each other. She has said in the past, "My problematic ideas are my favorite ones"—the idea that unpicking our own problematic thoughts should be encouraged, not silenced, and that is how change is made.[24]

CONVERSATION IS A TWO-WAY THING

Sometimes we definitely hear things. Paul and I moved into a new house, and a week in, with the back doors open, he said, "Do you hear that? That high-pitched sound?"

"No," I said.

"There. There! You didn't hear that?"

I shook my head. This went on for a while. He was frustrated that I couldn't hear it. I wanted to hear it; I was trying, but I just couldn't. It was a strange realization that some of our hearing is tuned differently. Some people can hear higher-pitched sounds than others and therefore their reality is different from those who can't hear them. Similarly, one weekend recently I was sitting outside a countryside hotel having lunch and there was a guy and girlfriend sitting at a table. She said something about her dress being black. He said it was blue. She said it was black. This went on for ages. They asked the waitress and she said it was more of a blue. I turned to have a look, and I thought the dress looked black. A simple example of how sometimes we do see things differently, and maybe we won't ever know for sure who was officially "right." Maybe it doesn't matter who was right. So many conversations don't work online at the moment. Are we really trying to tackle politics, racism, inequality, climate change, in 140 characters? In a back-and-forth comment section? No wonder we end up getting frustrated and blocking each other.

I remember someone once saying that when two people speak, they are having two different conversations; that is how dialogue in a book often reads—two people having separate threads of thought. Often, we don't really listen to what the other person is saying; we are merely patiently waiting for our own chance to speak. It's something I try to check. When I read Julia Cameron's book *The Listening Path*, I realized how important properly listening to someone is because we rarely do it. Properly listening to someone, hearing them out, not waiting to speak, is basically the closest we can get to what love is—making someone feel seen.

I kept hearing about this new app called Clubhouse, an audio-only platform where people can host "rooms" and people take turns to speak. Sounds good enough, but I personally was put off by too many "gurus" talking about how they had manifested their money or people claiming to be shamans while having massive egos. Clubhouse grew rapidly in popularity, and one day an online concierge service emailed me offering to monitor my account until it was my "turn to speak" in a room. So, you can now pay people to "monitor" conversations until you get to broadcast your bit? Ick. It gave me a funny feeling. Has social media turned into this? A place where we used to connect is now being treated as just a place to wait until you get to speak? Because that is the opposite of listening. If we forget how to properly listen, we are in danger of completely disconnecting from each other and living in a world of individual egos floating aimlessly around. That would *not* be good. It's time to listen.

EMAIL LIKE A PERSON

First off, I'll admit I really enjoy the automatic Gmail reply when I'm very busy. Dashing off a "Great, thanks!" can be useful when in a rush. But recently I've been amazed by the way people send emails. An outreach manager recently sent the most strangely robotic email:

> *I emailed you a short while back but didn't manage to inspire you enough to respond. I'll make it so easy that you'll barely be able to stop yourself.*
>
> *Please, reply with one of these:*
> *1 = Leave me alone, or Unsubscribe.*
> *2 = I'm interested, please send me the media pack.*
> *3 = I'm not sure at all. Contact me again in a few weeks.*
> *I'm really keen to start working with you.*

This isn't an email I feel inclined to respond to. It's not how real people talk. It's so mechanical. Why are they telling me what to reply with? I would have much preferred if someone said, "Hello, how are you? Here's a thing you might be interested in because of XYZ." Elizabeth Gilbert has said in the past that coming into someone's inbox is like coming into their house. You don't just go into someone's house uninvited. It's not rocket science to be more friendly human, less dry robot when speaking online.

OPEN COMMUNICATION

The thing about social media is that it's full of stories with most of the information missing. We see photos and pixels and our brains try to fill in the blanks. By doing so, we are almost fabricating the details in our own minds because people aren't showing the full picture. And as discussed earlier in this book, it's not always because we're trying to be mysterious; it's because it's simply difficult to express our true selves through a screen. A few years ago, I noticed that someone I thought of as a friend had unfollowed me online. Not a close friend but someone who I had worked with a few times and saw out and about. I couldn't help but be hurt by it and privately brainstormed all the reasons why she had unfollowed me. I decided to do what you're "not supposed to do" and just reach out and ask her about it (something I probably wouldn't do now). She said it was an "accident" and we moved on from there. But something didn't feel right. A couple of months later I got a message from her out of the blue. She explained that she had been in a bad place lately, having had a new baby, and while trying to work out how to perform a "career pivot," she was feeling vulnerable. She didn't want to see someone (me) seemingly having it all together online. The irony was that, during that time, I was having a big anxiety flare-up—I was struggling to sleep and was not in a great place myself. This open communication made us feel better. It was the nature of the app to just shut down and push away from each other when perhaps what we both most needed was someone to admit the truth to. We should absolutely unfollow and delete whoever we want. But it's also worth knowing that if you are the one being unfollowed, and you are triggering someone unknowingly, it's never really about you anyway.

HOW TO HAVE A BETTER CONVERSATION

1. First, context is key (i.e., the circumstances that form the setting for the conversation, panel, event, statement, or idea, and in terms of which it can be fully understood). Lay it out.

2. Don't immediately go on the defense or personally attack someone if you disagree. You can disagree with someone without lowering yourself to making personal remarks about them.

3. Remember the conversation has to have two sides in order for it to be a conversation! No monologuing at length. If someone starts doing so, gently say, "You're monologuing," and be aware when you are doing so yourself. Let the other person speak. Try to have equal airtime.

4. Commit to clarifying what each person actually means when you feel yourself making assumptions—ask someone to clarify things and get specific.

5. Let them know you understand and acknowledge their point in the parts where you do (even if this only means

the smallest of crossovers in points of view).

6. Remind yourself and others that you can disagree with someone or an element of the discussion without needing to completely wipe your hands of them. *Most* people do have a basic level of goodness and can change their minds or come round, maybe after they have had time to think. Disagreeing with them does not necessarily mean disliking them.

7. Jamie Bartlett recommends, however hard it might be, assuming the "principle of charity": "Try to view your opponent's argument (or loved one in this case) in the most charitable way you can. Too often we do the opposite. Always assume they are as smart, knowledgeable, thoughtful, and well-meaning as you consider yourself to be. On that basis you'll find at least interesting points of disagreement rather than all the noise."

8. It's hard! But so worth it. Why not have a conversation with someone today (friend, family member, acquaintance) who you've disagreed with in the past and have an honest conversation about it?

THE ART OF CRITICAL THINKING

"Social media: where an emotive anecdote that
confirms your biases is the purest form of truth."

—@jamiejbartlett

JUST LIKE "THE ALGORITHM" WAS ENDLESSLY SUGGESTING THINGS I
should buy, I felt people on the internet (strangers and friends)
were constantly telling me what to think. I don't mind a sugges-
tion of a good moisturizer for sensitive skin, but suggesting who I
vote for, for example, riles me up. Sometimes we follow along with
a trend or popular way of thinking without asking any questions.
It's OK to ask questions. This isn't about rocking the boat for the
sake of it, and I am a believer that the devil already has enough
advocates, thanks. But it's OK to zoom out occasionally, and
check in with yourself—ask yourself: What do you *really* think
about that? Are you afraid of being shunned from your social
group if you disagree? How much is your thinking your own?

It can be confusing, and frightening even, being told what
to think all day every day by strangers, friends, or brands.

As children, we are open-minded; we aren't yet socialized or influenced to think a certain way about the world. Children are mostly kind and believe in fairness, not because someone told them to but because it's human nature. Are there ways we can "unlearn" and get back to questioning things properly, digging into what we truly think again? I asked Tom Chatfield about it. He's someone I really respect in this field and is the author of many books, including his latest, *How to Think*. He answered, "One of the wonderful things about having a child is how it can transform an ordinary activity or everyday event—going to the shops, taking a walk around the block—into a whole universe of noticing, exploring and questioning. If you let it, it can give you permission to pay incredibly close attention to countless tiny things your adult mind filters out. And it also connects to the astonishing lack of assumptions that characterizes children's questions about the world. They question everything, they take very little for granted—and this is the perfect way to start thinking about, and then rethinking, what's going on in your life."

I tell Tom that sometimes before I formulate a proper opinion myself, I check Twitter to see what the consensus is first. I think I am thinking for myself but then no doubt get a bit swayed by the popular opinion (of my social circle). How do we challenge ourselves further to think critically outside of our bubble? He replied, "Social media can be a brilliant way of testing the waters, of seeing what's out there in terms of ideas and opinions and feelings. But it can also lead to the kind of self-censorship you describe, where the crowd in the cloud signals what it's legitimate to feel and think about a particular issue—and what kind of tone and ideas it's OK for someone like you to hold. One way of pushing back against this is to diversify the backgrounds and ideologies of the people you follow on social media, to seek out eloquent advocates of positions you disagree with. But it's even more important, I would say, simply to spend plenty of time engaging with slower sources of information: to read, watch, and listen serendipitously, and then to give yourself enough time and space for your thoughts to take on their own forms."

I like this advice, on opening yourself up to differing opinions and slowing down. The problem was I was becoming so fatigued and cynical about the online culture wars and the fact that no one seemed to be listening to each other. People would seemingly rather box themselves in, giving themselves such strong social or political labels that it was hard to know what these people really thought or the impact they made in their day-to-day lives or what we really agreed on outside of the labels and moral signposting. I asked Tom, Is there a way to question things and people regularly without becoming cynical of absolutely everything? Or should we be? He said, "I think it's worth making a distinction here between three things: cynicism, relativism, and constructive doubt. To be cynical is to be reflexively dismissive of everyone else's motives and claims: to assume in advance that everything is being done for an ulterior motive. To indulge extreme relativism is to assume that every point of view is equally valid, so there's no meaningful

way of preferring one thing over another: Anything goes. It's easy
to indulge both of these tendencies—but it's my belief that you're
much better off trying to doubt things constructively. This means
taking a close interest in the limitations of your own and others'
understandings and in what it means to engage critically, but also,
crucially, in how knowledge can be acquired and tested, despite
these limitations. In other words, it's about using doubt as a path
towards surer understanding."

I asked him for any tips on how to share an opinion that
differs from those you love. Did he have any tips on how to have
better, deeper conversations with close family members you
don't agree with? He said, "Having good conversations is, first
of all, about establishing a context within which an empathetic
exchange can take place in good faith." This is important, I
think. The exchange of understanding and empathy—seeing
the argument not as a "me vs. them" but as two people trying
to make sense of the world and feeling safe enough to discuss
it with each other. He recommends really trying hard to shut
up too: "Let others speak. Try truly to listen to what they are
saying, and to work out what they mean. Don't make it all about
you." It's amazing what happens when you let someone fully
speak and not fight to be heard. If in doubt, always be curious.
Ask "What makes you think that?" instead of immediately going
in for the attack if something jars you.

Jamie Bartlett, author of *The People Vs Tech, The Dark Net,*
and *Radicals Chasing Utopia*, is another wise voice on the topic

of critical thinking. When I spoke to him, he made a great point that critical thinking doesn't need to mean "question and doubt absolutely everything": "The problem with critical thinking is that alone it can simply lead to 'question everything' and conspiracy rather than a proper study of epistemology. At the root of it all, though, is probably concentration and attention. These skills or assets should be viewed in the same way as fitness or diet. Something to be worked on throughout life." This is definitely something I am going to continue to work on, like Jamie says, over the course of my life. This definitely isn't about being so open-minded you end up on countless conspiracy websites(!), but it is about zooming out occasionally, gently questioning before consuming, and seeing each other as human beings instead of digital avatars who are constantly out to get us and constantly wrong about everything. It's about questioning ourselves too. There is absolutely nothing wrong with a bit of constructive doubt.

THE ART OF COMMUNITY

*"It's about people. First and foremost, community
is not a place, a building, or an organization;
nor is it an exchange of information over the
Internet. Community is both a feeling and
a set of relationships among people."*

David M. Chavis and Kien Le,
What Is Community Anyway?

FOR ME, THE HEART OF BUILDING A COMMUNITY IS TO NOT ONLY
create space to enable more connection but also to make
people feel safe. Sadly, so many areas of the internet make
us feel unsafe, and that is made better or worse depending
on our structural societal privilege. It is a side effect of an
unwell society when instead of communities, we have cults,
people finding belonging in online "communities" that foster
hate—from gossip forums to "incel" culture (a subculture of
misogynistic men). A few years ago, I interviewed the incredible
Laura Bates for my podcast, with the question: "Do we need

an internet police?" She said, "We need an internet system that actually takes this seriously. The justice system has to catch up, whether that means an extension of the e-crimes unit, whether it means better training for other police forces; but I think we also need to be able to demand that social media networks who want to use women as their customers and make a profit from them actually put their money where their mouth is and protect them." Laura's incredible network Everyday Sexism really sticks out as a way we can use social media for genuine empowerment. It acts as a support system, an activist network, a way to get people talking and also gathering data on the truth of the matter when it comes to sexism in our everyday lives. For example, she said, "A woman from Peru can send us a tweet that someone has just groped her in the street or shouted at her from a van, and within moments there will be women from India, Poland, Germany who have seen that tweet, checking if she's OK, supporting her. In many ways it helps us feel part of this international movement." This is the good, supportive side of social media—which is needed especially when it is possible to get two hundred rape threats and death threats in a single day, which is what Laura herself experienced for just doing her job. You'd think by now we'd have a rigorous system in place on social media to stop this from happening, but we don't. But in the meantime, we have to look out for each other and make each other feel safe wherever we can.

SOCIAL "ME"DIA

Individualism is on the rise, according to published findings from the Association for Psychological Science.[25] Focusing on ourselves, in many ways, is good—caring about ourselves and our own mental well-being is important; looking inward at how we can be better can be beneficial. But an increasingly individualistic society is defined as people who are self-serving, narcissistic, and not caring too much about the impact their individual decisions make, catering to themselves over and above other people. Collectivist cultures, on the other hand, see the importance of connection with others, community, embedding ourselves in a wider social system and context—and want to focus on relationships, family, and working together. My work and lifestyle setup could be seen through the lens of being individualistic: I work for myself, I love independence, I like spending time alone, I do believe each and every one of us has unique superpowers that should be harnessed. *And*, I am concerned about the rise of individualism, very skeptical of the "I don't need anybody!" mottos spouted by solo entrepreneurs. We all need each other. No one can navigate through society and not need anybody. The clickbait Instagram posts that say, "You don't need anyone" and "I'm the CEO of my own life" make me feel a bit queasy. It's arrogant to think you could exist entirely in a vacuum of your own creation. It shouldn't be a badge of honor to feel as though you can be totally self-sufficient without needing help from anyone. Perhaps we may want to feel as if "we've got this" by ourselves, as a defense mechanism, but we all need a community and each other. The food we buy, the art we consume, the bricks that were laid to build the home we live in, the parks we walk through—we need so many more people than we think.

FINDING YOUR PEOPLE

Is there a difference between a "tribe" and a "community"? I like the definition written by consultant and author Alan Weiss: "Communities are inclusionary. They are characterized by common attitudes, interests, and goals. Religion, beliefs, kinship, and opinions can differ starkly in communities and, in fact, give them vibrancy and dynamism, allowing for continued experimentation and growth." Communities can be full of like-minded people and slightly differently minded people; at least that's the goal. People often say, "Find your tribe," but tribes are more exclusionary by nature.

The thing with having a very close tribe—a group of people who need you to do certain things in order for them to accept you—is that it can be very intoxicating. Elizabeth Gilbert wrote an essay on Facebook, based on the teachings of Dr. Mario Martinez, and it blew my mind. It's why we find it so hard to tell our parents that we want to change careers, why it's hard to say no to going to a party when all your friends are going, why it's hard to go against the grain and say something different on Twitter. In very extreme circumstances, it can even lead to truly horrific things like "honor killings" when young girls are killed by their own family members. That is how much can be at stake for some people to leave their tribe of origin. On the less severe end of the scale, when we leave our tribes, we often get punished in some way: ghosted, deleted from an online group, cast out, accused of "disappointing" the family, or socially piled on. And it can still be very difficult, and even damaging to our mental well-being. But when you leave a tribe that is no longer serving you, you are coming back to yourself. As Martha Beck says, if you are finding your "way of integrity," then you're on the right path to truly finding your people and yourself.

THE SMALL THINGS

As Olivia Laing said in a recent *Vanity Fair* interview, "It's not self-care I'm hungry for, it's being part of a community, the give and take of regular human life."[26] Sometimes it really takes the smallest steps to start to build more of a community spirit, online and offline. Online, it can be reaching out to someone you've been thinking about. In an interview with *Stylist* magazine, Rebecca Seal explains that she would "sit on the doorstep with a cup of coffee and watch people go by. . . . I've got to know the people who live on my road much better, and now the woman who lives opposite me comes out and has a chat. It sounds like such a small thing, but it's been so uplifting—I just take my coffee out and drink it on the doorstep, and it just makes me feel connected." Social media can be a lifeline for anyone going through serious bouts of loneliness or depression of any kind. It's not as clear-cut as "social media makes us feel disconnected." There have been plenty of times when watching a YouTube video or connecting with a friend online has gotten me out of a funk. For people with chronic illnesses, they socialize from their beds, and it is extremely meaningful. For people who have moved to a new place or new country, social media can be the place to meet new people in their area.

COMMUNITY BEYOND CORPORATE COMPANIES

It is a lovely thing when people come together over their love for a celebrity. It is a very specific type of fan forum where people bond over their shared love, and it's a space to fully geek out over someone important to you. These spaces seem easier to enter for people—an inviting place to be a fan. But I agree with writer Haley Nahman, author of the *Maybe Baby* newsletter, who wrote, "We need less celebrity- and brand-worship and more opportunities to build connections from which no one person or entity stands to profit over the rest, where our connective tissue goes deeper than consumption preferences, and where trust enables mutual understanding and healthy conflict."[27] We have more power than we think to set up our own communities, for ourselves, without needing to be told which communities to join. As Sarah Drinkwater said to me,

"We've been stuck at home for a year. It's solidified the dominance certain companies like Amazon have. So, it's easy to feel that that's the way things are . . . but nothing is set in stone. Every action you take is a vote for how you want the world to be. Maybe for you that means shopping in the cute independent bookstore or deleting your Instagram account or starting your own small-scale social network just for your friends—the point is it's your choice." If you could start your own small community, what would it be about or based around?

CUTTING OUT THE MIDDLEMAN

It excites me that a Wi-Fi connection and a good idea can reach people. In 2019, I interviewed Emily Weiss, founder of Glossier, for my podcast show *Ctrl Alt Delete*. I remember being totally bowled over by her quiet determination, confidence, and focus. Weiss launched a blog, *Into The Gloss*, which then released products and has now turned into the juggernaut that is Glossier. Lots of big chains/malls in the United States were desperate to stock her products, but she shrugged. She didn't need them. She had the internet and a "buy" button. Thousands of people (read: young millennials) would preorder Glossier merch through the website before it went on sale. I kept thinking about this and how it is also how the influencer economy operates and will continue to operate. But we are all influencers now. This isn't about someone on a beach selling bikinis to a million followers. This applies to someone who is wanting to start a stationary line, or a life-coaching business, or a consultancy—and to get started, all they need are a few people who are genuinely interested in the service. Direct-to-consumer. It works for people as well as companies. The rise of Patreon, for example, and writers being able to deliver their words directly to an audience of readers who pay a small monthly fee and where creators can earn good salaries. Instagram consultant Sara Tasker runs online courses to help people grow their Instagram presence and makes a killing. The San Francisco newsletter company Substack connects writers with paid subscribers who read their words. And my personal favorite, The Pound Project, whose founder JP Watson came up with the genius idea to sell mini books full of interesting essays. For £1 you receive an online link, and for £5 a paperback book. It's a beautiful, successful way to monetize writing, removes the middleman, and empowers creators to be paid fairly for their work.

We are desperate for community again, and there are online communities cropping up that are not so positive. Hate forums, for example, where the common bonding ground is how much they hate influencers or hate other mums or hate women. Are we really lacking human bonds online so much that we feel the need to drag each other down in order to have something in common? Reflect on your own online communities—are they places of positive or constructive discussion?

ASK YOURSELF: IS SOCIAL MEDIA ENHANCING MY REAL LIFE?

My rule for internet use was to always check in with myself regarding this question: Is it enhancing my real life? Are my online connections people who bring something to my offline life too? Do the accounts I follow inspire my home or day-to-day life? Do I have a platform and want to make change? Do the apps I use have an impact on my life (e.g., the Nextdoor app—online I can see what my neighbors are posting, which translates into real life as it enhances our IRL relationships)? Right now, I am enjoying Instagram accounts of interior design because they inspire me to make my real-life space more relaxing. I want my online and offline lives to have a harmonious, positive relationship. I want my online life to influence my offline life for the better.

BUILDING A COMMUNITY: PRACTICAL PROMPTS

"Authenticity often equals attention, which equals value, which equals prosperity."

—Martha Beck

WHAT'S MISSING?

The best question to start with is to ask yourself or friends what is missing—what community is currently not available to you? What discussions or resources would help you more in your day-to-day life? It could be as niche as you like. For example, would you love a community of fellow freelancers to discuss pay/invoice chasing? Would you like to set up a Jilly Cooper–themed book club? Would you love to start a gardening community in your local area? Would you like a jogging group or partner? Would you love to meet more people who have the same breed of dog as you? Start by writing down the community you'd love to join, and if it doesn't yet exist, you might just be the perfect person to start it.

START SMALL

On an episode of Elizabeth Gilbert's podcast *Magic Lessons*, Glennon Doyle spoke about the power of community and how she built hers. She spoke of when she first started her Instagram page and had fourteen followers. She said, with absolute sincerity, that she showed up "for those people, the same as fourteen thousand." You focus on those people, the fourteen people who are showing up for you. She said, "You don't try and get more followers. You serve those followers so well that they invite more people in." It becomes a natural, organic growth, not because you're trying to build followers but because you're building a community that people find enjoyment and value in.

USE THE INTERNET TO DO THINGS IRL

It seems we've forgotten the core function of social media, which is to actually be social. Speaking to author Cate Sevilla about the old days of Twitter, she reminded me of Twestival, the global Twitter-based fundraising event. What does she miss about the internet from ten years ago? She said, "Meet-ups with people you follow (or larger events like Twestival) happening and for it to be normal." For me, it feels like social media isn't fulfilling the initial promise of actually being "social." When I occasionally do meet up with internet friends in person, it's a wonderful feeling to connect with people who you get such feelings of connection with online too. Is there anyone you enjoy speaking to virtually who you haven't seen IRL for a while?

GET "SNUGGLY"

Bear with me here—this is something inspired by my career coach Selina Barker. Getting "snuggly" means going smaller, bringing people in with you closer, instead of emp ty broadcasting or focusing on appearing "shiny." It means engaging in a more intimate way through messaging, Facebook groups, newsletters, podcasts—a space online where you feel like it is a two-way dialogue and a hub for people to interact and connect. It seems to be "the norm" to use social media to broadcast our achievements and try to turn ourselves into mini superstars, only showing the shiny side of life. Since becoming more "snuggly" online and treating it as a place to share and be vulnerable, my experience on social media has become so much better. Of course, I choose what to share, but I'm not trying to perform anymore.

BIGGER IS NOT ALWAYS BETTER

The author Paul Jarvis wrote a book called *Company of One* that I found eye-opening and refreshing. It's all about building a genuine community and how being entrepreneurial doesn't have to mean "scaling" at speed and growing bigger and bigger. His idea of building a company and community centers around focusing on your existing customers or followers—serving them properly and avoiding the temptation to grow for the sake of it. What is your definition of success when it comes to growing a platform online? He reminds us that real connection rather than increasing followers is often better for business and better for us as humans.

DIGITAL CITIZEN CHECK-IN: NINE QUICK WAYS TO CONNECT WITH YOUR COMMUNITY

1. Reclaim your morning. Prioritize yourself first thing in the morning, instead of diving straight into the chaotic online world inside your device. Starting the day feeling grounded helps you be a more solid support for others.

2. Join an app like Nextdoor and take it offline—make connections in your local area, even small things like giving away items you no longer need or noticing if something looks unsafe.

3. Send a nice message to someone you cherish. Who haven't you spoken to in a while that could use a nice word of encouragement?

4. Arrange a meetup. Reach out to some people you know and admire and ask if they'd be interested in meeting up and discussing how you could make something close to your heart better.

5. Have an uncomfortable conversation with someone. Instead of blasting someone publicly with assumptions, send a direct message to someone you slightly disagree with and have a conversation on why you disagree and why it makes you feel uncomfortable.

6. Amplify someone else's message. Don't speak for or on behalf of anyone. Choose a cause, issue, thing, or person that you want to amplify—online, in the pub, or just walking down the street. Choose to amplify something you feel is important (e.g., a local park having a tree cut down, a petition, an important story) and share it, not because it makes you feel good but because it is an action that you can include in your daily practice. And always credit the source—if you are sharing a piece of content or information online, always credit the creator.

7. Find new causes you can donate to—be it your time, money, or skill set. Getting involved offline is even better.

8. Report anything dangerous online there and then. Social media has a long way to go in terms of making users feel safe, especially more vulnerable citizens or those in any sort of minority group. Use the "report" button. Stick up for people in danger. Reach out. Write a letter or email—

getting in touch with your local leaders will never be wasted or regretted.

9. Follow and donate to Glitch, an award-winning UK charity founded by Seyi Akiwowo that is working to end online abuse—particularly against women and marginalized people. It is an incredible source of information on how to be a better digital citizen.

NOW WHAT?

THANK YOU FOR PICKING UP THIS BOOK AND READING IT. I DON'T
have a big revelatory conclusion for you, I'm afraid, but I
hope some of the ideas and tips in this book might inspire
ways in which we can disconnect from what isn't serving us
and connect to the things that make our lives more joyful and
meaningful. Now's a good time to take stock of what the internet
has given us, and how we want to continue using it. We are at
a tipping point culturally of how we decide to continue using
this mammoth tool that is part of our day-to-day lives. We can
continue to get lost in it and feel weak in its tight grip, or we can
unleash ourselves and decide what purpose we want to have.

I hope you can take some time out to rediscover who you
are again away from all the noise, find your people online and
offline, have conversations with people who challenge you, and

find or build your own community. And I hope you are never too embarrassed to be curious or change your mind. I do worry that we are drifting away from each other under the guise of perfection and distraction and that our engrained social media habits might be making us flaky friends. Let's reboot. Get creative for creativity's sake. Reach out to people more. Make things even if no one sees them. Dig deep and notice the causes that need help beyond the headlines. Connect with like-minded and not-so-like-minded people. Scrap the shiny exterior of the personal brand. Show the real you. Let's connect beyond a like button. Please do say hello.

ENDNOTES

1   https://e360.yale.edu/features/exploring_how_and_why_
trees_talk_to_each_other

2   https://www.mayoclinic.org/healthy-lifestyle/tween-
and-teen-health/in-depth/teens-and-social-media-use/
art-20474437

3   https://www.oliverburkeman.com/so/14NZw7Z07
?languageTag=en&cid=51b6978e-c2af-4d65-a12e-
82fc8941cc96#/main

4   Simon Sinek, *The Ted Interview* podcast: https://www.ted.
com/talks/the_ted_interview_simon_sinek_work_is_
never_going_back_to_normal

5   https://www.inc.com/john-brandon/these-updated-stats-
about-how-often-we-use-our-phones-will-humble-you.html

6   https://juliacameronlive.com/basic-tools/morning-pages/

7   https://www.huffpost.com/entry/work-life-balance-the-90_b_578671

8   https://www.npr.org/2021/03/16/977769873/the-age-of-automation-is-now-heres-how-to-futureproof-yourself

9   https://www.facebook.com/groups/290368045246716/

10   https://www.independent.co.uk/life-style/gadgets-and-tech/facebook-inventor-deletes-app-iphone-justin-rosenstein-addiction-fears-a7986566.html

11   https://www.nts.live/shows/literaryfriction/episodes/literary-friction-7th-october-2019

12   https://medium.com/consensys-media/how-i-fell-out-of-love-with-the-internet-1a8d3f9dc0c3

13   https://www.instagram.com/p/COnuqQTti_f/

14   https://www.marketsandmarkets.com/search.asp?search=influencer+marketing

15   https://www.prweek.com/article/1590362/majority-uk-instagram-influencers-engage-fakery-landmark-new–study

16   https://www.forbes.com/sites/laurenfriedman/2017/02/08/millennials-and-the-digital-experience-getting-your-digital-act-together/

17   https://influencermarketinghub.com/influencer-marketing-statistics/

ENDNOTES

18 https://www.wired.co.uk/article/social-media-future-sharing

19 https://www.wired.co.uk/article/whatsapp-alternatives-vs-signal

20 https://magculture.com/blogs/journal/danielle-pender-riposte-1

21 https://www.creativelivesinprogress.com/article/handsome-frank-instagram

22 https://www.instagram.com/p/BwcjMbAAZQE/?hl=en

23 https://www.irishexaminer.com/opinion/columnists/arid 40286819.html

24 https://www.theguardian.com/culture/2019/feb/26/ayishat-akanbi-my-problematic-ideas-are-my-favourite-ones

25 https://www.psychologicalscience.org/news/releases/individualistic-practices-and-values-increasing-around-the-world.html

26 https://www.vanityfair.com/style/2021/05/olivia-laing-well-then-wellness-diary

27 https://haleynahman.substack.com/p/36-community-fandom-or-cult

ACKNOWLEDGMENTS

THANK YOU TO THE THREE HUNDRED–PLUS PEOPLE I HAVE interviewed on the *Ctrl Alt Delete* podcast over the past five years. The conversations we have always go back to how we can stay curious and connect more deeply with each other and the world around us. Thank you all for your generosity and time, and for inspiring me to write this book and live my life differently. Thank you to Allison Adler, Kirsty Melville, Cat Vaughn, Briony Gowlett, Abigail Bergstrom, Viola Hayden, Kim Butler, Lynsey Routledge, Justin Girdler, Selina Barker, Huw Armstrong, Zakirah Alam, Sahina Bibi, Vero Norton, Oliver Martin, Elizabeth Garcia, Diane Marsh, David Twiddy, and Devon Ritter. Thank you to my husband, my friends, and my family for your support, always.

ABOUT THE AUTHOR

EMMA GANNON IS THE *SUNDAY TIMES* BESTSELLING
author of *Sabotage*, *The Multi-Hyphen Life*, and
Olive. She is the host of the No. 1 careers podcast
in the UK, *Ctrl Alt Delete*. She lives in London.

 Enjoy *Disconnected* as an audiobook narrated
by the author, wherever audiobooks are sold.

Andrews McMeel Publishing
a division of Andrews McMeel Universal
1130 Walnut Street, Kansas City, Missouri 64106

www.andrewsmcmeel.com

First published in 2022 by Hodder & Stoughton (UK).

22 23 24 25 26 VEP 10 9 8 7 6 5 4 3 2 1

ISBN: 978-1-5248-7059-1

Library of Congress Control Number: 2022930759

Editor: Allison Adler
Art Director: Diane Marsh
Production Editor: Elizabeth A. Garcia
Production Manager: Cliff Koehler

ATTENTION: SCHOOLS AND BUSINESSES
Andrews McMeel books are available at quantity discounts with
bulk purchase for educational, business, or sales promotional use.
For information, please e-mail the Andrews McMeel Publishing
Special Sales Department: specialsales@amuniversal.com.